The Neuroscience of Business

Series Editors
Peter Chadwick
Ideas For Leaders
London, United Kingdom

Roderick Millar
Ideas For Leaders
Edinburgh, United Kingdom

Neuroscience is changing our understanding of how the human brain works and how and why people behave the way they do. Properly understood, many of these insights could lead to profound changes in the way businesses interact with their employees and customers. The problem is that, until now, most of this research has been published in specialist journals and has not made its way to managers' desks. At the same time, however, business leaders and managers are faced with a plethora of extravagant claims based on misunderstood, or exaggerated, neuroscientific research. Palgrave's The Neuroscience of Business series seeks to bridge the gap between rigorous science and the practical needs of business. For the first time this series will describe the practical managerial applications of this science in an accessible, but in-depth, way that is firmly underpinned by a clear explanation of the science behind the management actions proposed.

More information about this series at
http://www.springer.com/series/14428

Shane O'Mara

A Brain for Business – A Brain for Life

How insights from behavioural and brain science can change business and business practice for the better

Shane O'Mara
Trinity College Dublin
Dublin, Ireland

The Neuroscience of Business
ISBN 978-3-319-49153-0   ISBN 978-3-319-49154-7 (eBook)
https://doi.org/ 10.1007/978-3-319-49154-7

Library of Congress Control Number: 2017939698

Cover design by Fatima Jamadar

Printed on acid-free paper

This Palgrave Macmillan imprint is published by Springer Nature
The registered company is Springer International Publishing AG
The registered company address is: Gewerbestrasse 11, 6330 Cham, Switzerland

Preface

In the course of the journey we are going to undertake in this book, I invite you to open your mind to a whole variety of possibilities that discoveries in the modern brain and behavioural sciences have provided us with. I invite you to take advantage of these discoveries and to attempt to use the knowledge that you've gained to make your workplace, your organisation, a kinder, gentler and, above all, a smarter place to work in.

Neuroscience—the science of brain and behaviour—has emerged as one of the key and exciting sciences of the twenty-first century. It is the science that explores the mechanisms that create you as a thinking, feeling and behaving individual, and of us, as humans. In this book, I gather together adaptive and practical insights from the behavioural and brain science to changing business and business practice for the better.

Overall Goal of the Book: To bring adaptive and practical insights from brain science to change business and business practice for the better. *Why?* Because the brain matters in business: without a brain, you have no business. The brain is the most complex structure in the known universe. The brain is responsible for each of us being conscious, being able to think, feel and behave. The brain is also profoundly plastic and can change for the better or worse as a result of experience.

Underpinning Vision of the Book: Applying recent research on brain function and behaviour to people within organisations and workplaces—and especially knowledge workers. Our brains have many biases, heuristics and predilections, and we know more about how to work with these than ever before. Behaviour change is hard. Adopting tactics and strategies that are well founded in the science of brain and behaviour can help individuals and organisations to adapt to the demands of the modern world.

Hoped-for Impact of the book: Redefining the way businesses incorporate brain sciences into their culture, strategy and operations in a measurable and reportable way. Additionally, to provide a focus for generating new capabilities and ideas of significant commercial value to participating organisations. We will attempt to extract from the vast body of data that has been generated in the behavioural and brain sciences over the past few decades, applications and findings of specific use and application to business practice, development and management.

Many conventional treatments of organisational life (broadly conceived) ignore those aspects of human behaviour that are founded on the shared similarities of brain structure and function between individuals. Our starting point arises from the simple reality that our behaviour arises from the structure and function of our brains. We then proceed by examining a series of brain-based ('neurocognitive') analyses of common aspects of human behaviour relevant to business and management practice. The range of topics being actively researched within neuroscience now is quite remarkable, and neologisms are appearing to label the research effort responsible for the fusion of these topics. Neuroeconomics, for example, is emerging as an important discipline, as the sciences concerned with brain function, decision-making and evolutionary psychology (particularly those aspects of evolution concerned with altruism and altruistic behaviour) all begin to merge within a common theoretical framework. Social neuroscience is another new and important endeavour that seeks to understand how social behaviour is generated by the brain and how the brain manages and is changed by social interaction. The wonderful catchphrase 'from neurons to neighbourhoods' has been used to summarise this new science—investigating the social brain.

Caveat Emptor: I define neuroscience here as the science of brain *and* behaviour. A reasonable and not uncommon reaction among some neuroscientists is to say that there is no overlap between neuroscience and business. Nonetheless, there is some gap in the market for ideas and practices being filled by people who offer services in neuromarketing, brain-based leadership and the like. Some will object and say that much of what passes for neuroscience in business is actually psychology, which, in and of itself, is not particularly a deep problem. The problem in this case is more one of the appropriate label. The definition I offer emphasises brain *and* behaviour, and it is one that explicitly disparages a silo approach to the creation and generation and indeed application of new knowledge. The phrase 'brain and behavioural science' captures this repudiation of a silo-based partition of knowledge pretty well. An analogy might make things clearer. It is likely that you, as the reader of this book, have purchased a car, or a computer or even a simple mechanical device such as a bicycle. Most people—not all, but most—want to know more than where the driving position is, steering wheel and brake, or whatever. They want to understand what goes in the engine in addition to being able to drive the car. They want to know the optimal fuel to feed the car to to power it appropriately. This important sense of having some knowledge of what the brain is and how it functions under particular circumstances can be both enlightening and useful. Having respect for the performance constraints of a car's engine, driven by some knowledge of how that engine works, is useful to every driver. So it is with the brain. It is responsible for generating cognition, for generating mood, for generating behaviour, and the attempt to place a neat dividing line between the knowledge of one discipline and another in the interests of some form of disciplinary purity is entirely contrary to the spirit of human enquiry and an ethos of interdisciplinarity.

The choices presented here regarding the topics to be presented and discussed focus on areas where we have some understanding of the underlying brain mechanisms and some understanding of the cognitive or other mechanisms that are present. The balance varies, depending on the focus of the particular chapter. We will see, for example, that understanding the brain's mentalising network provides an astonishingly useful rubric for how we, as humans, engage in person perception and brand perception. In other cases, the dual focus on brain and behaviour is less strong. This is particularly so in the case of behavioural design for de-biasing judgements about others. No doubt, however, in another few years' time, some useful and interesting experiments will have been conducted that provide a blend of behavioural and brain levels of analyses. Where knowledge in a particular area is incomplete, it simply indicates that there is a research agenda to be tackled. It also means that when you, as a reader, encounter particular claims regarding applications of brain science within business, some scepticism may be appropriate, and a toolbox for sceptical thinking is provided in Chapter 1.

Acknowledgements

I toyed with the idea for writing a book like this over quite a few years. A few false starts, and much discussion and encouragement later, the book was finally underway. The delay turned out to be useful—or at least I rationalise it as such—as much of the literature I have been able to cite and discuss here simply did not exist or was in too immature a state to be useful. Things are advancing rapidly now, and books like this, which deliberately try to steam-roller disciplinary boundaries, are now possible.

I owe many people thanks for this book eventually emerging: Maura and Radhika, for all the reasons you both know; my family and extended family, especially Lorinda and Myles, with whom I have had many (surprisingly!) useful conversations. Thanks are also especially due to Dr Tara Swart for introducing me to Roddy Miller who gave great encouragement to this project through many emails and discussions; Stephen Partridge, my editor at Palgrave Macmillan for giving the book the go-ahead. Others provided encouragement and useful discussion at differing points—Vincent Walsh; Laurie Knell; Tara Swart. Lynn Scarff and Ian Brunswick of Science Gallery Dublin kindly supported the 'Brain for Business' lectures in the Science Gallery Dublin, and Jess Kelly of NewsTalk provided expert moderation and hosting of the events. Thanks are also due to the co-presenters and discussants (especially Stephen McIntyre and Aoife Lyons) as well as the attendees at these events for sharp questions and comments. I have also had many useful conversations with many colleagues in a wide variety of organisations and businesses—from academic and research, pharma, finance, law and accounting, clinical and tech (I won't name the individuals to spare their blushes). Two blogs have been immensely useful to me, by providing alternative viewpoints on all sorts of business-related matters: *Flip Chart Fairy*

Tales—wonderful for deconstructing the world of work and organisations—and *Stumbling and Mumbling*, for providing an alternative perspective on economic matters. Susan Cantwell provided wonderful secretarial assistance.

I also thank the Wellcome Trust and Science Foundation Ireland for their generous support of my research through the years. Trinity College, Dublin-The University of Dublin also deserves particular thanks for continuing to be a wonderful institution and a great place to work. As usual, any mistakes in the text are mine alone, and I apologise for them in advance.

Contents

1

A Background Scenario from Organisational Life

The Meeting and the Final Negotiations

Mind your own business (English proverb)

There are many industries that one could choose for the purposes of pre-senting the story to follow, but here I choose an industry that I have long observed, namely the pharmaceutical industry. Novel and selective drugs are essential to my research work on the ageing brain and occasionally have proved very useful for the relief of minor headaches or other minor ailments! The pharmaceutical industry has many problems: competition for highly-qualified scientific staff, the high cost of bringing new drugs to the market, the risks of unexpected 'adverse events' caused by those drugs when adminis-tered to patients in a litigious society, a product pipeline that lacks new blockbuster drugs, a product development life cycle that can extend over decades, competition between companies for market shares and, increasingly, very severe competition from vendors of generic drugs when blockbuster pharmaceuticals come off patent. A wave of consolidation between many of the large pharmaceutical companies has taken place over the past two decades or so; this is a trend that is likely to continue. Opportunities for consolida-tion have revolved around finding partners that make logical sense in terms of the eventual goal of bringing novel drugs to the market. Do the potential partners match in terms of product pipeline, production facilities, novel bioassays, product distribution, logistics, cost-control and innovation? Is there hidden value in the large library of compounds, molecules and other

© The Author(s) 2018
S. O'Mara, *A Brain for Business – A Brain for Life*, The Neuroscience of Business, https://doi.org/10.1007/978-3-319-49154-7_1

agents that most of the pharmaceutical industry possesses? Will the eventual company have an internal and external logic that makes sense to investors, regulators, prescribers and patients? These issues are very complex and are difficult for one person to grasp in their entirety; in an important sense, mergers of these multi-billion dollar or euro entities with their tens of thousands of employees involve a complex act of faith, vision and facts.

The Background—A Fictional Case Study

Several months of meetings, offers and counteroffers have taken place, all of the relevant issues have seemingly been worked through and today is the day the final joint memorandum of understanding and intent signed by the negotiating teams, draft contracts agreed and the final actions listed in order for the three businesses to be merged. The stock analysts will then be briefed and the regulators informed.

CEO Profiles

Tom Spengler, late 50s, overweight, face flushed, has been CEO of Alphapharm for 15 years and believes there is nothing he doesn't know about his company or the pharma industry; the merger today is to be his legacy for the future. After all, combining the businesses will allow them to combine product lines, pool revenues, enhance research and development activities, and allow a single marketing and advertising line. Only good can come from this, Tom believes, and he has worked the numbers to prove it—or rather, his handpicked financial analysts ran the numbers for him. This was his chance to make good the loss of face and the loss of money on his previous merger attempt with another pharma company— one that betrayed him in the end.

Jim Johnson, early 40s, trim, fit and CEO of Germane Biotech, originally founded on spinoffs from his research work at a leading university hospital, is ambitious, driven and knows that he doesn't know enough about the pharma industry. He is also cautious and knows how to read a balance sheet. His years in biotech have led to him to be cautious about supposed new opportunities. He is especially adept at focusing on downside risks, having been involved in several failed large-scale clinical trials.

Mary Kearney, mid 40s, accountant by training, CEO by vocation, was a recent surprise appointment to head Levenson-Herbert Pharmaceuticals after many years spent in the music industry, another industry with a rapidly changing business model and collapsing revenues. She knows how to read balance sheets, and her training in a major accountancy practice during a period when it merged with difficulty with another major practice. She particularly understands that the future is not a continuation of the past— that businesses need to be especially careful that they are not overtaken by technological changes that come seemingly from nowhere.

The Companies

All three pharma companies are mid-ranked by market capitalisation. Tom expects, on the basis of *his* numbers, that the merged entity will be worth more than the three companies would be if kept apart. Tom has chosen his numbers carefully in order to make the strongest possible case for the proposed three-way merger.

The Opening

Tom, Jim and Mary enter the boardroom ahead of their teams, with Jim and Mary speaking quietly to each other. Tom strides ahead of them; this is *his* day, a day to create a legacy. His mouth is a little dry, and his heart is beating a little faster than usual. Some twinges in his chest he attributes to stress. He feels, as he likes to put it, good stress—stress to keep him on top of things, to keep his edge. Jim and Mary are smiling a little, and their hearts are beating quickly, and their breathing is faster than normal. Curiously, neither of them has really looked Tom in the eye when they were shaking hands, but he hasn't really noticed. He hasn't noticed that their conversation is largely directed to each other, rather than him. But then, he has other things on his mind…

Tom has worked very hard for this day: spotting the initial opportunity, negotiating with his board, selling them the idea, working the numbers, eyeballing all the legal documents. He has directed his team from the start, driving them hard, and making sure they were informed on a need to know basis—which wasn't much, because, after all, he, Tom, was the visionary. He was right to keep driving ahead and push his team in this direction—he was paying them enough! And for the ones who questioned his numbers and judgement—well, they were disloyal and jealous, just wanting to stop him grabbing his moment in the sun. Just as well he got rid of them! A good team is a unified and obedient team, directed by a strong leader who knows his own mind. A good team player knows they have a job to do, and they should, indeed must do it, and it alone. That is what they trained for; they shouldn't fool themselves that they can learn to do other jobs. He mulled again on the logic of the merger. All the companies are of a similar size, and there seems to be a good strategic fit and an excellent business case to bring them together. They all have the same core market, but bring different strengths. Germane Biotechnology has a very strong research and development unit, which is generally regarded by observers as industry-leading. Alphapharm has a very strong logistics and distribution network and is well diversified around the world. Levenson-Herbert has a well-branded market presence and is exceptionally adept at sourcing new and competitive suppliers for their production line, allowing them to keep costs under control and their margins on production industry-leading. All in all, as far as Tom is concerned, merging the three companies promises a combined future in sales and growth potential that far exceeds the organic capacities of any of the individual companies alone.

The Meeting

The teams sit around the table; Tom at the head and Jim and Mary beside each other, with their teams positioned to their sides. Jim and Mary both reach for the water on the table in front of them; their mouths feel very dry now. They are both perspiring more than usual and are glad the air-conditioning is turned to a lower temperature than normal. Jim chews on his pen; Mary is twirling her hair repeatedly between her fingers. Both are tapping their feet underneath the table. They glance occasionally at each other, holding the look with blank, emotionless faces. Tom doesn't notice anything out of the ordinary about his partners' behaviour; he is hardly paying them any attention at all. He quietly chews on a caffeine pill and is glad that he has a nicotine patch in place—he doesn't like to smell of cigarettes at these meetings. The caffeine helps with the fatigue—Tom has been sleeping very poorly for some time and hardly at all last night. Hard to keep your head clear when you're sleep deprived, but maybe his team will jump in when he needs them to…

Tom calls the meeting to order. His attention is focused on the page containing the short meeting agenda; although he prepared it 24 hours ago, he can barely remember the contents of it now. His heart rate has risen, and he can feel his heart beating in his chest. The stakes are very high: multiple millions are at stake between the merged businesses, and Tom wants to position himself at the head of the merged entity. He is not so concerned about positioning Jim and Mary in the newly merged company. In fact, Tom has never really discussed this with his partners; he assumes they will be happy with the positions that he has chosen for them. After all, nobody would be here but for him. He picks up his pen, fumbles it, and almost immediately drops it again. Nerves, he thinks.

'Welcome all', he says to the assembled group, noticing that his tongue sticks to the roof of his mouth and feels as if it is too large for his mouth. His heart is beating more rapidly. He tries to focus on the agenda and fidgets with some of his assembled documents; he looks around and says, 'We have a short agenda today—we must agree the final shape of the deal, assemble the relevant numbers, and...and...' Why won't the words he thought he had practiced come? He pauses, his breathing coming in shorter and shorter bursts; he is convinced that everyone must be able to hear his heart; it is beating so loudly. He stumbles and mumbles on '...agree, agree the draft of ah, ah, eh, final...joint memo of recommend, eh recommendation to our boards and our share-holders...'

That was not so good, he thinks. Still, the assembled teams are nodding in agreement. He starts to speak again and the words flow a little more: 'We have the chance to achieve something great here today, bringing together our businesses'; he relaxes a little, thinking that his tongue seems not to be so large and his mouth not quite so dry. His heart rate has slowly a little too, although the twinges in his chest are still present.

Just as he about to continue, Jim and Mary raise a hand. Mary speaks. 'Tom, many thanks for bringing us together today. We have all worked hard to get here, and we all greatly appreciate your effort and your hard work.'

Tom nods appreciatively. This is after all just the truth of the situation. Without him, they would have nothing!

The Left-Field Move

'Tom, before you go further, there is something we need to put on the table.'

Tom looks around, surprised and curious.

Mary continues calmly: 'We've looked very carefully at your numbers, and can't make them stack up. Not really. They conceal a lot of wishful thinking, and the imputed values for goodwill and reputation are, very frankly, non-sensical. You've made far too many assumptions about future cash flow, and you've ignored the negative effects that diluting shareholding is likely to have on how the market will perceive this deal. Your assumption that we can do a down-the-line debt-for-equity swap to refinance the deal is completely untested. Moreover, in governance terms, far too much power and control is vested in a single individual—namely, you. We, therefore have deep concerns, and believe if a merger is to happen, it must happen on different terms to those you propose.'

Tom started to speak, paused, and lost his train of thought, burbling 'but, but, but…'.

Mary continued: 'So, Jim and I have made alternative arrangements. A merger is a reasonable idea, but it has happen according to a differing structure to the one you that you propose. We have agreed with your major shareholders—the pension funds that have been so very disappointed in your profits for these past years—that we will take over Alphapharm, dissolve it where possible, sell on assets that are free-standing to generate cash, keep the remainder and subordinate it within a merged Germane-Levenson-Herbert or GLH Pharma as it will be known. I will be CEO, and Jim will be Chair. You, I regret to say, will be out, but on very generous terms. Here are the documents laying all this out. You can sign at the various points indicated.'

The Aftermath

The ambulance arrived quickly. Tom lay there thinking that if you had to have a heart attack, a drug company headquarters was as good a place as anywhere. They had stolen his company from under him too, he thought. Why hadn't he given them greater consideration and tried to see things from their perspective? Too late now. Will I make it alive to the hospital, he wondered, as the medical team stabilised him in the ambulance.

Exercise

1. List the thoughts, words, and phrases that occur to you regarding:

      i. Tom's leadership style

    ii. The effectiveness of Tom's leadership style
    iii. Tom's stress levels
    iv. Tom's methods for coping with his stress levels
    v. Tom's insights into the motivations of other people
    vi. Tom's health behaviours and self-care

2. What lessons have you learned?
3. What would you have done differently from Tom?
4. What do you think of Mary and Jim's tactics?
5. Which of these people would you work for? Why?

2

Scene-Setting, Background Information and Tools for Thinking

The brain is a wonderful organ. It starts working the moment you get up in the morning and does not stop until you get into the office.

(Robert Frost 1874–1963, Poet)

The guiding principles of this book are that '*knowledge is power*' and that '*to be forewarned is to be forearmed*'. These clichés have a point: to be aware of and to take active strategies to thwart say, pervasive cognitive biases that affect how we all make decisions, are vital and possible. As a result, decision making in business (perhaps under pressure and with poor or insufficient information) may therefore be much more effective. Another important lesson of this book is that the common idea of the brain as hard-wired and therefore immutable is simply incorrect. The key lesson of modern brain science is of the astonishing plasticity of the brain—that it is in fact the most plastic organ in the body. This capacity is referred to as 'neuroplasticity'. The components of the brain are remodelled, reworked and sculpted by experience—including the experience of reading this text! It is by capitalising on this capacity for change by individuals that business cultures can adapt, learn and evolve. Leveraging this capacity for plasticity also allows changes to become ingrained and instantiated within the culture of the business itself.

© The Author(s) 2018
S. O'Mara, *A Brain for Business – A Brain for Life*, The Neuroscience of Business, https://doi.org/10.1007/978-3-319-49154-7_2

At Your Desk

You're sitting at your desk as usual. The morning commute was not so bad, and you're looking forward to a busy and hopefully exciting week at work. The computer hums away quietly in the background, with emails pinging every few minutes; the mobile phone and landline are diverted to voicemail (but still give you visual alerts of calls arriving); the major report you will present to the senior management meeting at mid-day sits on your desk. Lots happening: you look about the office and watch your team. Everyone is seated at their desks, their facial expressions and behaviour all different. Some are smiling, some frowning, some blank. Some are assaulting their keyboards; yet others stare vacantly into space. If only you knew what was going on inside their heads . . . you wonder, what if you could see inside their heads? What would you see? You push the thoughts aside, as there is work to be done. You stand up, walk to the door of your office, open the door and loudly clap your hands together. A relative silence quickly settles as the faces turn toward you. You begin to speak, and they seem to listen.

If you could see inside their heads, what would you see? Inside, you would see a frenzy of activity: of molecules collected into cells, cells gathered into assemblies; assemblies coalescing into systems and systems tangled into brain-wide networks. And all of these in continuous communication together and with the outside world—the world that begins at the edge of the brain. You clapped your hands, and in under a quarter of second, the assembled brains stopped some of what they were doing, processed the sound, interpreted it as a signal to orient the heads and necks and body trunks they control toward you, to listen. To listen to what? The words and sentences you utter are just pressure-waves modulating the air; they are meaningless until they strike eardrums and are conveyed to the brain where they are turned back into words and sentences again. You have two, four, six, however many, brains with mutually co-ordinated activity. One making sounds—speaking, gesticulating, the others interpreting those sounds as words, sentences, calls to attention, calls to action. More than this, though, all of these brains are engaged in active housekeeping: keeping their bodies breathing, monitoring hunger, thirst, posture, sights and sounds, remembering facts and figures, stories, solving problems, negotiating positions on the social hierarchy, interpreting gestures and facial expressions. All these unique brains, housing individuality, personal history, ancestral history; all alike but all unique. This is a fantastical achievement and is perhaps the current supreme expression of the blind watchmaker.

All of this variation, difference, individuality, is vital, but it is not the whole story. We humans all share common principles of brain structure and function, and the modern behavioural and brain sciences are at last revealing some of these common structural and functional principles. We are starting to understand how people organise themselves into hierarchies and groups, how knowledge transmission spreads in groups, how humans reason and how they make systematic errors in reasoning, how the stress response occurs and how it can be managed, how we learn, remember and forget. We now have a vast wealth of information on how the brain manages conflicting sources of information, searches for unique items in a sea of similarity (such as how you identify your favourite brand of toothpaste quickly from among the tens or more brands available in the supermarket!), how fear and anxiety arises and how they might be controlled, even on how to give well-designed visual presentations (and to control the stress of speaking in public), given the limitations on human attention. We can also start thinking in systematic ways to apply this knowledge to our everyday lives.

Neuroscience Applied to Business

Neuroscience—the science of brain and behaviour – has emerged as perhaps the key science of the twenty-first century. It is the science of you as an individual and of us, as humans. The secrets of the brain are being discovered, and being discovered at a rapid rate. Topics that were difficult to understand or seemed to be intractable a few short years ago (e.g., who gets depression? Why? What are the most effective treatments for depression?) are getting intensive and revealing investigation, and slowly the functions of the brain are being revealed. In this book, we are attempting something a little unusual and new: we will try to extract from the vast body of data that has been generated in the behavioural and brain sciences over the past number of decades findings of specific use and application to business practice, development and management.

The range of topics being actively researched within neuroscience—the brain and behavioural sciences—is quite remarkable, and neologisms are appearing for to label the research effort responsible for the fusion of these topics. Here are a few: *neuroeconomics* is emerging as an important discipline, as the sciences concerned with brain function, decision-making and evolutionary psychology (particularly those aspects of evolution concerned with altruism and altruistic behaviour) all begin to merge within a common theoretical framework. *Social neuroscience* attempts to understand how social behaviour is generated by the brain and how the brain manages and is changed by social interaction. The wonderful catchphrase '*from neurons to neighbourhoods*' has been used to summarise this new science—the investigation of the social brain. There are many others: neuroleadership, neuromarketing, neurolaw and neuroethics are just some of the more popular portmanteaus of recent years. We will here explore a large variety of topics drawn from neuroscience of more or less specific application to business.

The regularities of human behaviour result from the shared similarities of brain structure and function between individuals. Explaining these regularities comes from these starting points: that these behavioural invariants derive from the fundamental fact of our existence—our behaviour arises from the structure and function of our brains. In turn, understanding these invariants should help make predicting and understanding what people do perhaps a little easier. It should also help avoid some of the commonest mistakes that are made in this very interesting and somewhat peculiar form of group and social life—the modern organisation.

Studying Brain and Behaviour in Modern Humans

The past few decades has seen a revolution in terms of the understanding of how the brain works, primarily because of the arrival of a whole new set of technologies that allow us to probe the structure and function of the brain. These technologies can be applied during both health and disease, and neuroscience is generating an ever-clearer understanding of both normal and abnormal brain function. Humans, unlike most other species, present special difficulties for the study of their brain and behaviour. Their brains are inaccessible in a way that the brains of other species are not; they may not be subjected to invasive investigation, with brain tissue harvested for further experimentation. Experiments on humans can only be conducted under carefully defined, controlled and regulated circumstances, and experiments involving controlled manipulations such as social or nutritional deprivation on the structure and function of the brain are generally not possible to conduct. Furthermore, the human genome has only recently been deciphered, but its meaning is still not clear: the day when each of us has our own personal genome deciphered and available to interrogate in a database is still some time away. Our knowledge of gene-gene interaction (the effect of one gene on another) or gene co-expression, or indeed gene-environment interaction, is still severely limited. At this point in time it is safe to say that there is little to no useful, actionable knowledge available on the level of the individual on these matters, but it is also safe to say that the next few decades will falsify this statement. What is clear is that any full account of human behaviour must fully account for the contribution of genetic factors and cultural factors to what is to be human; furthermore, the contribution of the unique psycho-socio-biological point through which these factors are developed, embodied and expressed—the human brain—must also be invoked, investigated and explained.

Human Cultures and Valuable Intangibles

Humans occupy the widest range of environments of any animal species on the planet: we are the only species living in the Arctic and the Antarctic, and we live in just about every environment between the poles. Even deserts have been and continue to be lived in by humans. Thus, the geographical environment of humans is remarkably variable: we have mentioned just a few different physical environments (think of the many, many other environments that humans occupy: the tropics, the rainforests, the dry plains of Asia, the rain- and storm-swept western coasts of Europe).

The cultural environments of humans are astonishingly variable, too. Comparing and contrasting the variation in population density, lifestyle, education, per capita income, immigration, occupational opportunities, and political, religious and social attitudes within the suburban USA is a fascinating exercise: comparing suburban California (say, the San Fernando Valley or Palo Alto) and suburban Alabama (say, Birmingham or Montgomery) brings this home. Now compare the similarities between Americans in terms of shared culture and the overlap between their culture and the culture of a nomad from the Kalahari desert, a refugee from a failed state (take your pick) or a citizen of a barely functioning and corrupt one (take your pick from the Transparency International listing) to a citizen from a state divided by social, religious and tribal behaviour (again, take your pick). We should properly expect that humans from these differing places will differ dramatically in terms of their expectations of the future, beliefs about the role of the state, and expectations regarding the corruption of state officials to the stability and independence of the legal system and of the judiciary. Finally, regarding the wealth and poverty of nations, what the World Bank (2006) refers to as intangibles ('human capital and the value of institutions (as measured by rule of law) constitute the largest share of wealth in virtually all countries')—perhaps up to 80% by their estimate. These intangibles vary dramatically between nations: in the developed countries of the world, they constitute perhaps more than twice the amount of wealth of developing nations. But where do the intangibles themselves reside? Intangibles, by definition, can't be touched or felt, but they exist. These intangibles reside in the behaviour, attitudes, culture, expectations, capacity for learning and change (adaptability) of the individuals within a nation. These capacities, in turn, develop from exposure through the lifespan to the educational, legal, ethical, political, religious and social institutions within these countries. In turn, these factors are instantiated within brains, and brains themselves have evolved over millennia to perform very differing functions. These include being survival- and present-centred in orientation, performing swift (but relatively fixed) learning from experiences of fear, stress and predation, and surviving in severely resource-limited environments.

The Peculiarities of Our Brains

Our brains also come equipped with a whole variety of cognitive biases, heuristics and predilections, designed to aid survival in these situations, all of which bias our behaviour in the very differing environment of today. Some of the factors making humans unique and different from other species include cultural transmission of values, behaviour, attitudes that occur during early development and upbringing (from parent to child; peer to peer; sibling to sibling). Added to this is, at least in developed societies, a sustained and long process of formal education—perhaps 20 years or more. This process of education builds on a remarkable capacity for learning, based upon a remarkably 'plastic' brain—perhaps the most plastic organ in the body. This capacity is expressed throughout the lifespan—and is not just something peculiar to the school years. The idea of 'life-long learning' has developing this capacity behind the policy stance.

Humans have another remarkable capacity—that of language. Language adds a dramatic complexity to the range and depth of interactions that we are capable of: if as a species we were sentient beings without the expressive capacity that language confers upon us, as a species we would not be, could not be, human. We would be something much closer to our non-human primate cousins. Language (and its remarkable offspring, reading) changes us into beings that have a future and a past, in addition to a present. Language changes us into beings that can express our inner brain states—our thoughts and feelings—as well as our past and our anticipated future brain states. Language can also fool us: its centrality to our behaviour and the close relationship between it and conscious brain states does not mean that language can provide a perfect read-out of the underlying brain states that generate it. After all, there are many brain states and behaviours that they generate that introspective language fails to describe or report in any meaningfully useful way. Try describing to someone without any experience of them how to ride a bicycle or a surfboard, for example; these are complex sensorimotor integration tasks requiring a strong element of implicit trial and error. Expert performance will derive from attempting the task and learning from doing.

Tools for Probing the Brain

The most popular and most underestimated and unrecognised tool for exploring the brain is language. Brain states (for example, knowledge of the past and present, one's behaviour, attitudes, biases) can be extracted by verbal probing or questioning. Humans are exceptional in the animal kingdom for having an astonishing capacity for communication that is directed forwards and backwards through time, and that can be used to reveal or hide intentional states, memories, fleeting thoughts and enduring dispositions. It is also the medium by which much learning occurs: the use of language can change the fabric of the brain. Structured explorations of brain states via questionnaires (for example, for political polling purposes; educational selection; evaluation of brain damage; occupational selection) are very popular and useful predictors of current and future cognitive, behavioural and brain states. However, one should not make the mistake that language can and does fairly, reliably and veridically reflect all, or even most, brain states. Much of our own behaviour is a mystery to us—if you doubt that, explain to someone else how you walk. Saying 'one foot goes in front of the other' isn't much of an explanation for this behaviour!

Traditional methods for exploring the brain involve exploring the anatomy of brain (usually post-mortem) or the neurochemistry of the brain (often by introducing chemical agents, such as psychoactive drugs) into the brain. Careful study of the effects of brain damage has also revealed much about the functions of differing brain regions. Invasive studies of the brain in non-human animals has also revealed much about the differing brain areas involved in different functions (such as seeing, appetite, hearing, the stress response, addiction, to name just a very few). New tools have been added to the traditional ones—the most popular high-tech tool of the present is probably magnetic resonance imaging (MRI), a tool that allows high-resolution functional and structural images to be taken of the living brain in action. MRI investigations are safe and non-invasive and relatively easy to conduct. The data extracted from them are, however, largely correlative rather than mechanistic, and experiments are usually conducted at the level of groups rather than individuals. At the current stage of development and knowledge, MRI is of no practical, *commercialisable* use for discriminating and predicting future brain states of individuals. MRIs are not a magic bullet that can detect the presence of lying, for example (for review, Chapter 3, O'Mara 2015). Other tools include the EEG (electroencephalogram), which provides a reasonably direct readout of electrical activity in the brain and is a particularly useful tool for probing certain clinical conditions. Genes implicated in brain function are being discovered at a regular rate, but these analyses are at the level of populations and are not yet, in general, useful at the level of making predictions for individuals. Again, the day when they will be is some time away, and the promise of personalised medicine, with pharmacotherapies tailored to your individual genome, is still some long distance away.

How the Brain Works: What You Need to Know

The brain, as is commonly observed, is the most complex entity in the known universe. It consists, just like every other tissue in the body, of cells. These cells are given the specialised name of neurons. These neurons have an unusual property: they form networks, and these networks have a particular function, which is the processing of information. This information can be of many types: what you're hearing, what you're seeing, the control of your breathing, the control of your posture, your plans and your intentions. All of those things comprise the kinds of information that is transmitted through the networks of the brain. Brain cells are unusual because they communicate directly with each other using chemical messages (the precise chemical details need not detain us here). The function of these chemical messages is relatively straightforward: it's to signal to other brain cells whether to fire or not to fire, and that's pretty much it. Brain cells, to a first approximation, are simple, and the language they use is simple. It's a language of excitation and inhibition, of firing or not firing. However, these signals have one remarkable property. These signals change the brain because the brain is plastic. By plastic, we mean that the brain changes because of experience—because of the patterns of activity that occur in the networks of the brain. The behaviours you engage in, the attitudes you have or adopt, the habits you have, what you think—all of these things can and do change the brain because the brain has this remarkable property of plasticity.

It used to be thought that during sleep the brain was much more quiescent than during the course of the waking day. Now we know that the brain never, ever rests, even during sleep. We now know, for example, that normal sleep is essential for learning and memory to function normally—skip a night's sleep, and you will lose the details of the important stuff from the previous day. The brain is remarkably hungry. It consumes about 20% of the energy available within the body. It has no energy stores. It therefore needs a constant and consistent delivery of oxygen to the brain, as well as glucose, which acts as the energy-producer for brain cells. The brain is hungry for something else as well, and that is stimulation. By stimulation, I mean the brain requires constant inputs from the outside world, or activity from within, generated by the networks within the brain, in order for it to retain normal functioning. This is one reason why we find boredom to be such an unpleasant experience. Recent clever experiments by Timothy Wilson and his colleagues (2014) have examined how hungry the brain is for stimulation. Students, left to their own devices in an impoverished room that contains merely a chair with a battery-pack shocker electrode, will, after a few minutes, start to give themselves small electric shocks in order to overcome the effects of boredom and thereby provide themselves with some stimulation.

The Brain Has Several Opposed and Interacting Networks

In what has to be one of the most important findings in neuroscience of the past two decades, experiments have shown that the brain flickers between differing networks of activation. When you are paying attention to a task (for example, reading the words on this page) a network, which is sometimes called the 'executive control network', is activated. This is a network that is situated principally in the frontal lobes —that is, the parts of the brain toward the front of the skull. However, when you allow your mind to drift away from what you are doing, to think about nothing, to mind-wander, to daydream, you suppress activity in the executive control network, and you engage activity in a network that is sometimes referred to as the 'resting state network' or the 'default mode network'. In our popular language we use phrases like 'an idea comes to mind' or 'I've just thought of something'. What does that thinking? When you perform some little bit of problem-solving, some bit of creativity, where do these solutions come from? It has recently been suggested that this flickering between this active state, which the executive control network is engaged in, and this default state, is the wellspring of creativity in the brain. A different way of thinking about this is that when you were engaged in doing 'nothing' or 'mind-wandering', you were allowing the brain to push into consciousness potential solutions to problems. There is a remarkable quote from the author Graham Greene, who writes as follows in his novel '*The End of the Affair*': 'So much in writing depends on the superficiality of one's days. One may be preoccupied with shopping and income tax returns and chance conversations, but the stream of the unconscious continues to flow, undisturbed, solving problems, planning ahead: one sits down sterile and dispirited at the desk, and suddenly the words come as though from the air: . . . the work has been done while one slept, or shopped, or talked with friends'. Greene hits on something very important here: that when engaged in difficult or creative work, or attempting to devise solutions to problems that are of their nature fuzzy and for which the solutions are ill-defined, feeding these non-conscious brain mechanisms through everyday activity, through information-gathering, through conversation, allows the brain to 'bring to mind' solutions that otherwise might be unavailable.

Systems of Thinking in the Brain

Daniel Kahneman (2011) and Walter Mischel (2014) offer us two very important ways of thinking about thinking and behaving. These are Kahneman's 'System 1' and 'System 2' and Mischel's 'hot' and 'cold' cognition. These ways of thinking about how we think complement each other and are metaphors—in other words, are not to be taken literally. But they do offer a useful rubric for understanding how we think and, in particular, how we can think better. Kahneman's System 1 and System 2 derives in large part from his work on 'cognitive biases'—the systematic deviations we often make from the rational and best course of action when engaging with a problem or making a decision. System 1 is fast, rapid, reflexive and is almost never without an answer. Hence, your ability to not 'not' think about a red elephant. The picture comes quickly and swiftly to mind, even if it is something that has never occurred in the real world. System 2 is different: it is slow, reflective and cogitates upon things, allows you to ruminate, even if excessively, on some decision or course of action. The interplay between these systems—a fast non-conscious system, and a much slower, conscious system, is what constitutes the contents of our cognition—the contents of our mental life. Mischel's model derives from a differing concern—how we control ourselves in the here and now, and over time. Are we easily provoked or do we easily ignore provocations? Can we control our tempers? Do we grab for the nice rewarding piece of cake now, or do we defer it, because we are concerned about our waistlines or our health? Mischel's model argues that there are two components to controlling or regulating our behaviour—a 'hot' component, which is action-oriented and seeks rewards now, and to hell with the long-term consequences. The 'cool' component, by contrast, opposes the actions of the hot system, tames it and is focused very much on long-term payoffs. The hot system grabs the muffin now, or at least wants to, and the cool system pulls the hand away. The hot system is therefore action-oriented, and the cool system is oriented toward repose and quietude. We will see in Chapter 3 that the hot and cool systems are distinct but interacting systems in the brain. Being conscious of these contrasts in how our brains work offers the possibility of insights into what drives us to behave in certain ways in certain situations and to offer important course corrections.

Evidence-Based Thinking: A Toolbox

Before we proceed further, it is worth considering the elements of evidence-based thinking. There are all sorts of crazy belief systems out there, and believing something contrary to the evidence can be dangerous and costly. Here are a few simple rules that should be used when considering whether or not to believe a claim someone makes. They might want to sell you a new learning development tool for staff training, for example. How do you know that they know what they are talking about? Try the following:

1. Always ask for evidence: any claim that is made must have empirical evidence associated with it. This is really the most important place to start from. No one should ever be embarrassed to ask for the evidence supporting an assertion, contention, decision or planned course of action.
2. Then determine what kind of evidence is being presented:

There are several types of empirical evidence that should be considered.

a. Evidence from epidemiology, where large-scale, unbiased surveys are taken of the population regarding a question of interest and an unbiased statistical attempt is made to determine the truth or otherwise of a claim.

b. Evidence from experiments where there is systematic manipulation of variables of interest and an unbiased attempt is made to determine the truth or otherwise of a deposition.

c. Evidence from randomised controlled trials (RCTs), where people are allocated randomly in a blinded fashion to treatment and control groups. For meaningful, evidence-based decision-making, RCTs are the gold standard and represent a level of sophistication in clinical decision-making that is essential in trials for therapies or interventions of any description in humans (see www.clinicaltrials.gov).

3. Then determine the quality of evidence:

a. Evidence presented in favour of a contention needs to be 'peer-reviewed' and published in a reliable scientific journal. 'Peer-reviewed' means that the evidence is tested by experts in the field and published in a peer-reviewed journal means that others can assess the evidence itself in an independent fashion so that it can be 'replicated'. It is only through a process of replication that we can be certain that a finding or set of findings is substantially true and reflects something of the real world.

b. Then ask—are the claims being made extraordinary? Is a supposed treatment being offered that would rid the world quickly of some scourge (for example, if it were to be claimed that 'serious clinical depression could be dealt within a day'). If the claim is extraordinary, the evidence required to support that claim must also be extraordinary.

c. Where has the evidence been published? Is it published in the normal communication channels, where it appears in the usual databases (for example, PubMed, Google Scholar, Web of Science) or is it published in some form of in-house journal? A good guide is from Martin Gardner's *'Fads and Fallacies in the Name of Science'*: some writers can be ... brilliant and well-educated, often with an excellent understanding of the branch of science in which they are speculating. Their books can be highly deceptive imitations of the genuine article—well written and impressively learned .... [but they] work in almost total isolation from their colleagues. Not isolation in the geographical sense, but in the sense of having no fruitful contacts with fellow researchers .... [they] ... stand entirely outside the closely integrated channels through which new ideas are introduced and evaluated. He works in isolation.

He does not send his findings to the recognized journals, or if he does, they are rejected for reasons, which in the vast majority of cases are excellent . . . [they] speak before organizations he himself has founded, contributes to journals he himself may edit, and—until recently—publishes books only when he or his followers can raise sufficient funds to have them printed privately.

d. How does the evidence fit into what is already known? We can determine this with reference to:

   i) The Cochrane collaboration (www.cochrane.org), an independent, not-for-profit assay of the evidence base for a whole variety of claims across the whole spectrum of biomedical sciences.
   ii) Does the evidence fit into a 'meta-analysis', where the overall pattern of reliability of statistical effect can be estimated?

e. Ethical reviews: does the evidence presented adhere to the ethical and other declarations that are required of normal human interventional studies (these included the binding Declaration of Helsinki 2014, ethics approval from an appropriately constituted ethics panel within an institution and the ethics declarations that are publicly available from the various medical organisations, psychological societies and others)? Studies conducted on humans require an extremity of care where ethical review procedures are concerned.

Any claimed intervention or supposed new body of knowledge that fails these tests cannot be regarded as part of the reliable corpus of human knowledge and should be treated with extreme care and extreme scepticism. These standards have been hard won over the last 100 years or so and are designed to ensure several things. First, that we do not fool ourselves with respect to any claim about any phenomenon. Second, that extreme care is shown in respect of any intervention that is conducted with humans. Third, to show that the knowledge obtained is reliable, generalisable and applicable across a wide range of circumstances. These are demanding standards to meet, especially in the case of claims about brain and behaviour. There is no end to the nonsense that people are willing to believe—often because there are cultural or organisational demands that trump reality (at least for a while). The pervasive acceptance that there are hard-wired 'learning styles' is one such belief: pervasive in many management consultancies and businesses, and completely and utterly absent from the empirical science of learning and memory, as a few minutes consulting the relevant scientific literature will tell you (see Chapter 6 for some details). Companies could save themselves money and time by distributing copies of a reliable and empirically well-founded book like '*Make It Stick*' by Brown and colleagues (2014). They could then simply not pay consultants who are telling them useless nonsense about how their employees are a mix of visual or kinaesthetic learners (or whatever). Similar strictures apply to the purveyors of nonsensical personality tests that are sometimes used for employee selection and analysis. Extensive empirical data support the existence of the 'big five' personality factors (Gosling and colleagues 2003: openness to experience, conscientiousness, extraversion, agreeableness and neuroticism, with the acronym OCEAN). The data do not support the fanciful dimensions of personality sometimes sold to companies for employee selection purposes. Similar strictures apply to the use of the polygraph (O'Mara 2015). The rule again is simple: ask for empirical evidence in the scientific literature from the purveyors of 'personality' tests that purport to be of use in an organisational context. If the evidence for efficacy can't be provided, then the 'tests' should not be used. The wonderful blog, *Flip Chart Fairy Tales*, has many examples of the kinds of nonsense that people within corporate life are willing to allow themselves to believe. A little gentle scepticism can go a long way (and save a lot of money too).

New Knowledge: Where Does It Come From?

Funding for the brain and behavioural sciences is provided by many national and international agencies, including the Wellcome Trust (UK), the National Institute for Health (USA), the National Institute for Mental Health (USA), the Howard Hughes Foundation (USA), the Allen Institute (USA), the European Commission (EU), the National Science Foundation (USA), pharmaceutical companies and med-tech companies. Success rates for grant applications in the behavioural and brain sciences are typically of the order of 2–10%. This means that the vast majority of proposals that are brought forward fail the grant agency's peer review process. This has two consequences: (1) it ensures that only the most excellent science is funded and (2) work that is not of the highest quality is not funded.

1. It is important to ask, in the case of any entity making claims regarding therapy or treatment, where its funding has come from and who is providing that funding. Funding through the charities and others just mentioned involves a rigorous process of proposal writing, peer reviewing,

ethical review and clinical, medical and institutional oversight. Where these are not present, warning flags need to be assigned to test the credibility of the claims that are being made.

2. Rapid progress is being made in the behavioural and brain sciences. The knowledge obtained is hard-won, but, for example, recent times have seen breakthroughs in the description of the genetic basis of autism, Alzheimer's disease, methods for harnessing plasticity in the brain to assist recovery after stroke, and so on.

3. Many novel tools have become available, including brain-imaging and genetic tools, among others. The overall question needs to be asked: if a body of novel claims is being made, where can and does it fit in this context? If it doesn't fit, if the rigour required to make a claim is lacking, if the ethical procedures required are not present, if the data are not published in the usual communication channels where claims can be tested, then considerable scepticism needs to be applied.

Over the coming chapters we will explore a wide variety of topics. We will show you, for example, how you make judgements about other individuals and how these judgements are snap judgements and need moderation to arrive at the best possible outcome, where, for example, employee selection is concerned. We will explore how, by focusing on the design of environments rather than focusing simply on individuals, we can make better decisions and to make these decisions more easily (so-called 'behavioural design').

We will also explore neuroplasticity—one of those now almost ubiquitous words that is widely used and abused, within both the behavioural and brain sciences and especially in the popular media. Probably the best way to think about neuroplasticity is this: the brain has a remarkable capacity for change. We know this because even in individuals who are suffering from the ravages of terrible diseases such as Alzheimer's disease, such people can still continue to learn new skills and new habits, even though their ability to consciously remember what they have just learned may be impaired. Neuroplasticity does not imply that you can suddenly and easily change your preferences, your proclivities, acquire a new personality or easily overcome the debilitating consequences of something like a stroke or a head injury. It does mean, though, that the brain retains a remarkable capacity to change for good or ill as a result of the experiences that it undergoes. In the context of the present book, neuroplasticity is a theme that sits behind much of what is to come over the following pages. But it does not mean that the deep fundamentals of how your brain is constructed can be dramatically altered. Rewiring of brain circuits happens on a local and micro level, and not usually or obviously on a large-scale or macro level. You will not grow a new lobe in the brain, for example. Therefore, the kinds of changes that you can engage in are likely to be the best outcome of a regular, reliable, systematic and incremental focus on a task or a problem. One of the key ways that we can change ourselves reliably is by focusing on the characteristic way we talk to ourselves about what our capacities and abilities are. It is becoming much more appreciated in recent years that self-talk has a key role in how we see ourselves, how we conceive of our own abilities, and how we can grow and change over time, and indeed how we interact with the world. The characteristic way we do this is referred to as a 'mind-set', and it is to this topic that we turn next.

Exercises

Make a list of the things that you need to consider when you:

1. Are determining the credibility and believability of an assertion
2. Think about how the behavioural and brain sciences may be applied in business and organisations
3. Think about how the behavioural and brain sciences should not be applied in business and organisations
4. List some business training practices that have no empirical foundation (this might require consulting some textbooks)
5. The limits of neuroplasticity applied to individuals
6. What lessons, if any, could Tom Spengler, our CEO from the prologue, have applied to how he ran his business affairs with regard to empirical thinking?

Readings

Big Five personality test—an online version http://www.outofservice.com/bigfive/
Brown PC, Roediger HL, McDaniel MA (2014) Make it stick: The science of successful learning. Harvard University Press, Cambridge, MA
Declaration of Helsinki (2014) World medical association: Ethical principles for medical research involving human subjects. www.wma.net/policy/
Flip Chart Fairy Tales – Business Bullshit, Corporate Crap and other stuff from the World of Work. https://flipchartfairytales.wordpress.com/ (updated frequently)
Gardner M (1957) Fads and fallacies in the name of science. Dover Publications, New York.

Gosling SD, Rentfrow PJ, Swann, WB Jr. (2003) A very brief measure of the Big-five personality domains. J Res Pers., 37: 504–528. http://dx.doi.org/10.1016/S0092-6566(03)00046-1.

Kahneman D (2011) Thinking, fast and slow. Farrar, Straus and Giroux, New York

Mischel W (2014) The marshmallow test: Mastering self-control. Little, Brown and Company, New York

O'Mara S (2015) Why torture doesn't work: The neuroscience of interrogation. Harvard University Press, Cambridge, MA.

Wilson TD, Reinhard DA, Westgate EC, Gilbert DT, Ellerbeck N, Hahn C, Brown CL, Shaked A (2014) Just think: The challenges of the disengaged mind. Science, 345(75–7). doi: 10.1126/science.1250830

World Bank Report (2006) Where is the wealth of nations? Measuring capital for the 21st century http://siteresources.worldbank.org/INTEEI/214578-1110886258964/20744844/Introduction.pdf

3

Mind-sets, Self-talk and Changing Behaviour

This chapter explores how the science of mind-sets and of self-talk provides a potential route to allow individuals to control and change their behaviour.

There is no expedient to which a man will not go to avoid the labor of thinking (Thomas A. Edison, inventor)

Learning Language and Using Language

Can you remember back to the age of three, or four or five? Can you remember the strangeness of learning that black marks on a page are associated with sounds? Can you remember how these sounds when put together became something you already knew—words? Can you remember something just as strange? Taking a small pencil or crayon or piece of chalk—something you used for daubing the freshly painted walls—and learning to make small movements on a piece of paper? These strange little marks—letters—had particular sounds associated with them, and when these marks were combined they did something almost magical: they made something that you already knew and used to control and manipulate your own world—words and sentences and stories. You probably can't remember learning to speak your native language however; learning your native tongue is as effortless as learning to read and write are effortful. Language is an astonishing capacity: once language learning starts children learn an average of

S. O'Mara, *A Brain for Business – A Brain for Life*, The Neuroscience of Business, https://doi.org/10.1007/978-3-319-49154-7_3

perhaps tens of words per day for years, to the point where they have a working vocabulary of maybe ten thousand or more words. These very differing abilities—speaking, reading and writing—all involve a massive and dramatic reorganisation of the brain, and they directly reflect how culture and experience shape and change the brain. This reorganisation as a result of being exposed to language and culture is possible because the brain itself is plastic.

Perhaps one of the greatest triumphs of modern neuroscience has been the finding that the brain is plastic—that it changes as a result of experience. Culture imprints itself on the developing brain, as does education, social experience and everyday life. Sometimes the traces of this imprinting can be enduring, sometimes not: experiences during the early years of life tend to provoke greater changes in the organisation of the brain. Learning to read and write causes widespread and more-or-less enduring changes in the structure, function and organisation of the brain. So much so that these functions become part of you. It is impossible for a fluent native experienced reader to see words and not interpret them as such, assuming your vision is normal. This is true in much the same way that the injunction 'think of a small furry dog' automatically elicits the image of a small, furry dog.

The Neuroplastic Brain

Formally, neuroplasticity is the capacity for the brain or its component parts to change as a result of experience, injury or development. The brain remains plastic throughout its lifespan, contrary to the old hard-wiring idea. The idea of hard-wiring may have grown out of the fact that it has been very difficult to demonstrate newly born cells in the brain—the number of brain cells you are born with is certainly vastly greater than the number you die with. We do now know that continued production of brain cells (neurogenesis) occurs in a limited number of brain areas—particularly in areas concerned with memory (such as the hippocampus). That is one type of neuroplasticity— new brain cells. Another type of plasticity results from creating or building new connections between brain cells, which changes how brain cells connect and communicate with each other through the differing and complex circuits of the brain. This process is brain-wide, and it continues throughout the whole of life. We now have very strong and compelling evidence that the old adage 'cells that fire together, wire together' is substantially true. Without this strengthening of connections as a result of activity, learning and memory would be impossible for a brain to achieve (Holtmaat and Caroni 2016).

This discussion is rather abstract—it is true in a trivial sense that the brain changes and rewires itself because of the activity that it, you, engage in. Is there an active way we can modulate this process? The growing answer is yes, at least in particular domains, by changing how we characteristically talk to ourselves about our abilities and capacities—our characteristic 'mind-sets'. We will focus here especially on applying neuroplasticity to yourself—by adopting a '*growth mind-set*' (rather than a '*fixed mind-set*') about your own potential. A 'growth mind-set' is a way of thinking that you are capable of learning across all domains. Mind-sets are inscribed in the brain and are detectable in the brain's electrical activity (the electroencephalogram or EEG). The good news is that they can be changed, and for the better. The changing mind-set approach—where the focus is on task and improvements based on effort—is scalable within organisations, as recent data very clearly show.

How and Why We Talk to Ourselves, and Why this Matters

The French philosopher Rene Descartes famously said '*Cogito ergo sum*'—I think, therefore I am. Descartes' point was that to prove you existed, you had to be able to think, and that the act of thinking implied an 'I' or an ego that engaged in that particular act of thinking. Going beyond this, though, we can ask: what is it that I think? What is the form in which thinking occurs? Is it in words, is it in images, is it in feelings, or is it in tastes, smells, or some combination of all of these senses? Just sit back, close your eyes for a moment and observe your thinking. Pay attention inward, but don't direct your attention in any particular way. You should notice that you have a continuous stream of thoughts, ideas, images and feelings, flowing through your consciousness. The act of paying attention to your inner life, the contents of your consciousness, as it were, is known as 'introspection'. Now push this mode of thinking along a little further. As you go about your daily life, do you talk to yourself? Do you talk to yourself a lot? Or not at all? As adults, we're usually at least a little embarrassed by being overheard when we are talking to ourselves out loud. We will apologise to others if we are caught talking aloud. Social mores sometimes suggest that people who talk to themselves audibly, in the presence of others, may not be in the best of mental health. I suggest social mores rather than psychopathological diagnosis, because, of course, children talk audibly to themselves, particularly between about the ages of three and eight or nine years, when their self-talk starts to become internalised.

Self-talk is actually a remarkably common feature of our mental lives and our behaviour. We are quite happy, for example, to note its existence in sports performers—John McEnroe, the famous tennis player, for example, was often heard speaking loudly in abusive terms to himself (and of course, he would often speak in strong terms to umpires and others). The psychologist Charles Fernyhough characterises thinking where we are engaged in some form of inner speech as a kind of a conversation, and this conversation may be replete with all sorts of words, telegraphic expressions and the like. This form of inner speech, of course, occurs in consciousness, and we are aware of it, and we are aware of contributing to it. And in contributing to it, we are actively changing the direction and flow of consciousness, and in turn we are aware of the change of direction and flow. This is not the whole story, however. Lots of mental activity happens outside the purview of consciousness. You, as the reader of this text, are not aware of the activity in the retina, or the other way stations through the brain, which convert little scratches or daubs on a page into words and sentences and meaning. The kind of mental activity that happens outside consciousness contributes to consciousness itself, because, of course, you are aware of the intrusion of the words that you are reading into your mental life.

Thought, Self-Talk and Behaviour

The relationship among thinking, self-talk and behaviour is not, by any means, straightforward. One very popular form of self-talk is a new year's resolution. It is an example of something that people may commit to publicly, but certainly will state they are committing to privately. They do so in the form of words, and more often than not they fail. They vow to give up cigarette smoking, or they promise themselves to cut down on the eating of chocolate. They promise themselves to get fit, join a gym, and then don't go to the gym after the first two or three weeks of January have passed. This failure of a verbal resolution involving behavioural change shows that there is no straightforward or close coupling between what we say to ourselves and what we do.

Here I examine self-talk as a phenomenon to provide us with a framework for understanding what self-talk is all about. Then, I want to set self-talk within a behaviour change context, focused on two well-founded methodologies from psychology and neuroscience: namely, rescripting or redirecting, and the induction of mind-sets.

Self-talk is a primary experience, in the sense that it is something that we are immediately aware of and can respond to. However, it is a private experience and the contents of self-talk may be something that we subject to a high degree of self-censorship or self-selection. We are all well aware, of course, of individuals for whom whatever thought happens to be in their mind appears to be blurted out, without much self-censorship (think Homer Simpson). Thinking is a covert, private activity and we all have a right to assume that the contents of our consciousness are not directly accessible to others, except insofar as we might describe the contents of our consciousness to others. Here, a note for the slightly paranoid: brain imaging machines, or indeed polygraphy devices beloved of police forces, especially in the USA, do not reveal the contents of your consciousness, nor indeed in principle, can they. My previous book (O'Mara 2015) deals with this topic in great detail. Here, it is sufficient to note that brain imaging allows you to visualise, in an averaged brain, in a group context, activations that are associated with particular brain regions or the network of activations associated with brain regions. The wonderfully coloured blobs that appear in brain imaging papers do not in and of themselves directly tell you the contents of the activity in that brain region. There is no need to worry at all about the existence of the lie detection machines that can reveal what it is that you are thinking, and organisations shouldn't waste their time and money exploring this possibility.

There are several methodologies for measuring what it is that we say to ourselves. Fernyhough deals with these in great detail, and I summarise the two principal ones here. The first involves '*experience sampling*', a technique that involves a randomly generated sound on a bleeper or on a smartphone and the participant simply recording what it was they were thinking about at that moment in time. The other principal methodology is that of the self-report inventory. In self-report, you attempt to remember what it is that you say to yourself under what circumstances, and you record your thinking or self-talk along a variety of differing questionnaire-specified dimensions. A central claim, which will feel introspectively correct to most people, is that self-talk is covert, private and has properties of free-ranging association that overt speech simply doesn't have. What we think and what we say are not the same. One way of thinking about inner speech is that it is a dialogue rather than a monologue. In other words, it is a debate, rather than a simple declamation or declaration. There are also forms of pathological self-talk. In major depressive disorder, sufferers will often report that their self-talk is very negative, in an evaluative sense, where they say to themselves that they are worthless, useless, hopeless or whatever. Pathological self-talk is also reported commonly in psychoses such as schizophrenia, but here the self-talk, in some sense, feels like it is outside the head, as if you are being spoken to. Fernyhough refers to this kind of self-talk as 'voice hearing'.

Why should we be interested in self-talk at all? A particular reason for being interested in self-talk is that it is one of the central aspects of our lived daily experience, and the way we talk to ourselves about what it is that we are doing, about what we intend to do or that we have done, may have important effects on how we regulate our own behaviour. In other words, by understanding and perhaps changing how we talk to ourselves, we might improve performance in all sorts of ways. Fernyhough (pp. 11–12) makes the key claim that 'inner speech....helps us to regulate our behaviour, motivate ourselves for action, evaluate those actions and even become conscious of our own selves...mental voices draw on some of the same neural systems that underlie external speech'. This is a very important claim, because it emphasises that the purpose, or at least a central purpose, of inner speech is to ensure that action systems in the brain are entrained, and behaviour is correspondingly generated.

Self-Talk and Performance

Self-talk has been examined in a variety of contexts. Among sports people, for example, it is thought to serve at least two functions. The first is a straightforwardly cognitive one, where you plan what it is that you are going to do now, and what you are going to do next. The second function is a motivational one, where you can engage in self-praise for a shot that has been properly hit or self-criticism for something that has been done badly. Here, self-talk engages error-correcting mechanisms. Finally, self-talk can consist of language and words that help you achieve a particular psychological state in order to perform appropriately and effectively. The key thing here is that self-talk has an important self-regulatory function, especially in contexts that are high stakes, such as sports competitions. The process of psyching oneself up is probably most easily executed in words, rather than in images. This latter possibility exists as well, but visualisation may require extensive training, whereas the appropriate use of words can narrow the focus of attention quickly and dramatically, which is a useful and central cognitive facet of self-talk. Self-talk during these high-performance events also allows some form of distancing from the self to occur, where the perspective adopted is of one person speaking to another, saying something like 'You've done this before; you can do this now; you can do this'. Here, the self is treated really as an object rather than a subject, and the dialogic or 'debate-like' quality of self-talk becomes very obvious.

Self-Talk and Planning for the Future

Self-talk supports planning of future behaviour, because you can construct and test a variety of counterfactual scenarios—counterfactual because they have not yet happened, but stating the scenarios out loud allows the testing of the scenarios against reality, and perhaps even estimating the likelihood they will happen. Taking these kinds of perspectives allows you, also through the medium of self-talk, to try and figure out what it is that somebody else might be thinking, or likely to do. In other words, to do that very human thing of trying to figure out what it is that somebody else is thinking, or likely to say. Scenarios like this, of course, play out in debates and negotiations where the key variables are to try and understand what it is that the opposing side might say, what moves they are likely to anticipate or how they might view a particular problem. Here we see that a key function of internal speech or self-talk lies in the understanding and managing of complex and potentially difficult social situations. Engaging in such covert speech also serves a protective function because it allows you to formulate plans and intentions without revealing them to your opponent.

What are the characteristics of internal speech that makes it so useful? Fernyhough and his collaborators claim that internal speech tends to be fast, it tends to be telegraphic in nature, and rarely, if ever, will it consist of fully formed sentences. It therefore is a very efficient form of, in Kahneman's terminology, system 1 thinking. The contents of the rapid search of memory and of pattern-matching are delivered quickly and very speedily into consciousness, and only then are they turned into external or audible words and speech. Simon McCarthy-Jones and Charles Fernyhough (2011), in an important survey of internal speech, suggest it has four principal properties. The first is that it is dialogic; in other words, it is a conversation between differing points of view and differing perspectives. The second is that it is condensed. The third is that it may have voices of people present, and the fourth characteristic is that it can be evaluative or motivational, where people use inner speech to assess what it is that they have done, or what they are about to do, and to provide energy to continue doing what it is that they may already be doing.

Brain imaging studies of internal speech are difficult to execute, but they have been conducted. 'Theory of mind' is our capacity to infer the mental life of other human beings, and a specialised network in the brain is activated when we consider what it is we believe others are thinking (the 'mentalising network'). Alderson-Day and colleagues (2016) show that the parts of the brain that are involved in Theory of Mind (ToM) are also the same parts of the brain that are involved in inner speech. It is reasonable to think that inner speech is supported, at least in part, by the brain's mentalising network, or that it provides input to the brain's mentalising network—that part of the brain that attributes agency to humans and indeed other entities such as cartoon characters or companies. We will meet the mentalising network again when we explore perception and brand perception in Chapter 5. We will now move from thinking about inner speech as the primary internal contents of consciousness, and think about how internal speech, when appropriately entrained, might manifest itself in changing behaviour.

Neuroplasticity, Brain Plasticity and Mind-Sets

Neuroplasticity (or brain plasticity) is the idea that the brain changes as a result of experience. It is also the idea that the brain changes as a result of the way the brain talks to itself, or, in other words, *how you talk to yourself about your interests, capacities and abilities*. This self-talk activates circuits and networks within the brain—this seems almost a tautology, but is worth emphasising nonetheless. People vary in how they see their own interests, abilities and capacities. This overall sense of how it is that you conceive of yourself is referred to as a '*mind-set*', a phrase, in its contemporary usage, we owe to the psychologist Carol Dweck. Dweck distinguishes two differing types of mind-set. The first is a growth mind-set, and the second is a fixed mind-set. A growth mind-set takes the view that your capacities, your abilities, your talents are malleable and that they can be improved through directed, focused and attentive practice. A fixed mind-set, by contrast, suggests that your talents, your abilities, your capacities are fixed. In other words they are immutable and do not change as a result of practice. We see this very commonly where people will say '*I'm not a mathematical type*'; '*I'm not an artistic type; I can't learn how to draw*'; or '*I'm not musical and I can't learn how to play a musical instrument*'. Similar strictures apply to how we interact with each other and especially how we speak to children. It's very commonly the case that parents will act to self-limit what their children are capable of by dismissing their abilities in a particular domain by saying '*Little Tommy isn't particularly sporting*' or '*Little Alice is no good at the piano*'. Children internalise these comments and will come to believe that they are, in fact, true. The key concept underlying the idea of mind-set is that those of us who regard our talents and our abilities as incremental and capable of being honed can show improvements in performance that do not appear in individuals who regard their own capacities and talents as entities reflecting an underlying, unchanging trait.

How to Change Mind-Sets

Dweck has conducted extensive observational and experimental work in a wide variety of populations, including populations that live and work in difficult or adverse circumstances, such as under-resourced inner-city schools. In one study, Blackwell and colleagues (2007) focused on achievement in junior high school. They administered a simple questionnaire to assess the degree to which people self-reported themselves as either having a fixed mind-set or a growth mind-set and then tracked academic performance over the course of the following two years. What they found was that those who self-reported as having a growth mind-set showed consistent semester-upon-semester improvement in academic performance, whereas those who reported having a fixed mind-set showed semester-upon-semester decline in performance. Now, you could argue that these are merely observational data, and you would be correct. There may be some other underlying variable that explains why there is a persistent difference between the academic performance of those with a growth mind-set and those with a fixed mind-set. That's why conducting experiments is important. In another set of experiments reported in the same paper by Blackwell, Dweck and her colleagues show that simple interventions can change a mind-set for the better. The interventions revolve around the type of feedback and praise provided by teachers to their students. Three types of feedback were encouraged, randomised according to the student type. The first is praise for a trait (in this case, intelligence) where the teacher would consistently say something like 'Wow, that's a really good score; you must be smart at this'. The second type of praise focuses on the behaviour and motivation, in other words, praise for the effort or process that the student engages in (for example, 'Wow, that's a really good score. You must have tried really hard'). And then the final group, the control group, get a simple piece of feedback saying little more than 'That's a really good score'. These students then are tracked over the succeeding period of time, and you find that students who are allocated to the effort group show an enhancement in performance in comparison to the control group and to the entity or trait praise group. This is a remarkably simple intervention. The focus is on providing appropriate feedback for meaningful effort engaged in, rather than simply providing praise for one's intelligence. The difference really comes down to the idea that students can learn that with focus and a determined effort to improve, they can improve, relative to where they were, compared with students who regard their performance as arising from a fixed trait such as intelligence, which they are unable to affect in any way. In this sense, consciously adopting a new mind-set by means of the feedback that teachers provide, or supervisors provide or, just as importantly, the way you speak to yourself is a radical act of self-defined neuroplasticity. Rather than saying to yourself 'I can't do it' because I'm not smart enough, you say to yourself 'If I work hard at this; if I focus on the problem, I can learn to get better'. And getting better, in itself, is a source of intrinsic reward—the kind of reward that comes with mastery of a new and difficult topic or domain.

Dweck provides a particularly dramatic example of the effect of praise for effort as opposed to praise for intelligence in a paper with a title that emphasises the theme of what has been said to this point: 'Subtle linguistic cues affect children's motivations' (Cimpian and colleagues 2007). In this study, Dweck and her colleagues focused on puzzle-solving performance in young children. Half were assigned to a group where they were simply praised for being smart during the course of problem-solving, and half were assigned to a group where they were praised for 'working hard' for solving the puzzles. Both children in both groups, of course, will feel pretty good about themselves, having been given such feedback. Now, the question is, how does that feedback subsequently affect performance? Dweck, in the second phase of the study, offered the children a choice of either a puzzle to solve or difficult or challenging puzzles to solve. What she found was quite remarkable. Of the children who had been offered praise for working hard, approximately 90% of them chose the difficult or challenging puzzles in the second phase of the experiment, whereas the majority of those praised for their intelligence chose the simpler puzzles. In a third phase, the children were then asked to solve mixed puzzles, difficult and simple puzzles, and the result still came through. The group that had been praised for working hard solved 30% more of the difficult puzzles compared to the group that had been praised for their intelligence, who actually solved 20% fewer of the difficult puzzles. This is quite some difference in performance, found in a group of seven-year-olds who were provided simple feedback about performance.

Mind-Sets in Work and in Organisations

In a managerial or organisational context, the lesson here should be clear: feedback, whether it's of the bullying type (you can't do this job because you're stupid) or of the supposedly constructive type (I haven't assigned you to this work group because I found you're not so good at doing these types of jobs) can actually be very destructive of performance. The lessons for managers, therefore, are straightforward. Managers should take the view that staff who aren't performing well on a particular task may not be performing well simply because the staff have not been trained properly for that task, not because they are stupid or lazy, or some other trait that is within the person. Managers, when they're providing feedback, should focus not on praising some underlying unobservable trait that is responsible for job performance, but actually focus on the behaviours that led to successful outcomes and on the outcome or performance of the job itself. This requires quite a shift in how many managers think about how feedback should be provided.

Mind-Sets and Activity in the Brain

Mind-sets are reflected in the underlying electrical activity of the brain. It is possible to measure the electrical activity of the brain by attaching electrodes to the scalp via a cap that is worn on the scalp and amplifying the signal that is obtained. The on-going electrical activity is referred to as the 'electroencephalogram' (or EEG). The consistent, over time, response of the brain to a particular stimulus (for example, a visual stimulus that might appear on a computer screen, a sound that from a speaker or a motor movement that the person makes) is referred to as an 'event-related potential' (or ERP). The ERP emerges when many trials are summed, one after the other.

Hans Schroder and his colleagues (2014) have shown that how the experimenter instructs the subject at the start of a simple task can have profound effects in terms of how the brain allocates resources to task performance. They chose what is known as a 'visual flanker' task. Here participants are presented with five-letter strings, for example, MMMMM or NNMNN, and the task of the participant is to judge whether the central letter (M) is the same as or different to the letters that flank it. If subjects are instructed at the outset that this is a task that it's not possible to improve on (in other words, that you are as good as you are and that's it) or that it's a task that they can improve on in other words, you can get better with effort and practice. You see a dramatic difference in performance and also a dramatic difference in the allocation of neural resources to, in particular, the awareness and allocation of attention to mistakes (the so-called error positivity component) during performance of this task. In other words, the language that is used by the experimenter has a very profound effect in terms of the underlying allocation of resources to task performance and task correction by the brain and also to behavioural outcomes. The lesson here should be clear: how managers, teachers and others who are charged with providing feedback can have a very important effect on task performance by individuals. Feedback that suggests, for example, that 'As far as I'm concerned you did badly on this task because you're stupid' is feedback directed towards an underlying and not directly observable trait, whereas feedback that's focused on an observable trait, for example, 'You did badly on this task because you haven't been properly trained and you haven't paid attention to the appropriate parts of the task' is much more likely to have a much greater effect on performance. Perhaps the key point to bring out here is that we humans are not just language-using animals, but we are social language-using animals, and how we use language with each other can have an important effect on subsequent on-the-job performance. This is so obvious that it shouldn't need to be stated, but it is characteristic of our interactions that we pay little attention to how our words are designed or not designed to enhance performance in the first place. So, subtle changes in the use of language by experimenters, by managers, by leaders, can have very profound effects on subsequent performance in a task.

Mind-Sets in Sport and Aviation

Does this kind of effect extend beyond academic performance? The answer is yes. In a study focused on observational learning, Andrieux and Proteau (2016) made an important observation about how we learn from others.

They focused on complex motor sequences (think, for example, how you learn a golf swing. You do so partly by observing others and partly by being instructed by others. Similarly, when you learn how to drive a car, you observe partly by observing others drive, but you also observe by being instructed while attempting to learn how to drive). What they found was quite remarkable. Participants observed models demonstrating a motor task at differing levels of competence and were given advance instructions stating the quality of the performance of the trials that they are about to observe (beginner; novice; intermediate; advanced; expert). Knowing in advance the level of performance and the classification of that performance markedly improves learning compared to being told after the trial was completed about the level of performance. In other words, the linguistic descriptor provided regarding the person that you are about to learn from has marked effects on subsequent learning of that task. The authors suggest that this form of prior instruction may prime the action observational network of the brain in ways that providing similar kinds of feedback after task performance does not.

The effects of how we speak to ourselves can be shown even more dramatically than the slightly prosaic example of learning how to swing a golf club. In an important study, Samuel Vine and his colleagues (2015) focused on pilot training. They had trainee pilots answer two questions about how they would deal with an engine failure occurring soon after take-off: this is one of the most dangerous things that can happen to a plane and requires considerable effort to re-land the plane safely. The trainee pilots were asked two questions. The first was 'How demanding do you expect the task to be?', which they had to score from 1–6, where 6 was extremely demanding and 1 was not at all. The second question was 'How able are you to cope with the demands of the task?', again similarly scored on a 1–6 scale. They then subtracted the first score from the second score to derive a simple measure of the emergency either as a challenge or a as a threat. A challenge is how the pilot perceives him- or herself as being capable of rising to the demands of the occasion, and a threat is where they have insufficient ability to cope with the demands of the occasion. What they found was that pilots who judged the engine failure soon after take-off as a threat performed worse across the board as compared with pilots who regarded it as a challenge. This was irrespective of actual performance in the simulator, or how a flight instructor, blinded to the condition, judged their performance, or how automated measurements of where they were looking to or gazing in the environment, or gazing at the control panel, were conducted. Again, this study does not go on to try and intervene to challenge the pilot's mind-set. But what it does do is focus on how the way the pilots conceive of their own capacities and abilities determines how well they are able to cope with an emergency situation and then subsequently to perform successfully or not in that situation. The lessons by now should be clear. How others speak to us and provide feedback on our performance, matters, but how we speak to ourselves about how we perform also matters. Focusing on performance, rather than on fixed traits, has a dramatic effect on our subsequent on-the-job performance.

Are Mind-Set Interventions Scalable Within Complex Environments?

One of the themes of this book is that the interventions that we can make within organisations to improve job performance and other types of performance can be relatively simple, straightforward and not costly. They should also not involve the investment of great amounts of time either to generate the intervention or for the intervention itself to be performed or for the assessment of the intervention's efficacy to become known. Here I focus on a simple and scalable intervention that may greatly enhance performance. One of the key problems with psychological interventions is that they take a considerable period of time to work. Experimenting with simpler, short forms of intervention is a very worthwhile endeavour. Dweck, with David Panesku and their colleagues (2015), has performed a scalable intervention on academic performance, involving approximately 1600 students in 13 geographically diverse high schools. The method they chose was simple and extremely cost-effective. They devised several straightforward interventions, as follows. The first was a single 45-minute online session that focused, using a summary article describing how the brain changes positively in response to a challenge; how it can grow and reorganise itself when students work hard and with focus on a task; and how neuroplasticity can enhance their performance on tasks that they would ordinarily see as being difficult. The students were also asked to perform two writing exercises. The first was to summarise the latest scientific findings on neuroplasticity in their own words. They were also asked how they would address a student who is becoming discouraged as a result of poor performance in school and what they would say to such a student about the importance of focusing on incremental changes in their talents as a result of motivated practice at tasks that they found difficult. Compared to controls, they found that the simple interventions just described enhanced grade point averages in high school students very substantially. Moreover, this intervention also reduced the chances of a student dropping out from high school very dramatically. The key point from a study of this type is that, with large workforces and good available online materials that have been prepared carefully with the focus on teaching the consumers of those courses what it is that they can change about themselves, can lead to profound enhancements in performance over the longer term. It is important, however, that the idea spurring a growth mind-set is not misunderstood. Offering praise for effort without emphasising the importance of focus, of attention to detail, to conscientiousness during task performance, and all the other variables that contribute to mastery, is pointless. Learners must understand that while what they are attempting might be difficult, they can improve their own performance, relative to where their performance used to be in the absence of paying attention to the components of successful performance. Dweck has suggested that merely telling your learners to try hard and to keep the focus on effort is just 'nagging'. The real point is to ensure that children understand that making an effort can be hard, but that adopting a metaphor like 'the brain is like a muscle' and that you must actively work it in order to see gains, is the best way to engage a growth mind-set. To reiterate, growth mind-sets shift attention away from individual traits and shift attention to the task and to learning. A growth mind-set, when effectively managed, emphasises the role of effort in creating talent. When Homer Simpson spoke to his children, Lisa and Bart, about a scheme of theirs that did not work, he said '*You tried your best and you failed miserably. The lesson is, never try*'! A growth mind-set is diametrically the opposite of Homer's. A growth mind-set helps maintain confidence and effectiveness, despite adversity, setbacks or challenges. The self-talk and behaviours involved in adopting a growth mind-set, compared to a fixed mind-set, result in a difference in the allocation of the brain's resources to performance on a task, especially toward monitoring for errors. Errors are a useful guide to learning because they provide feedback on where performance needs to be corrected. A growth mind-set interprets errors as being necessary for learning and providing the opportunity to learn. Thus, mind-sets can be conceived of as a form of radical, self-imposed neuroplasticity, because mind-sets can be taught, can develop as the result of what others say to you, but also, what it is that you say to yourself about your own capacities and capabilities.

Exercise

1. When giving feedback to staff (or indeed others—it doesn't really matter), do you focus on their behaviour—something that they can change? Or on their supposed character traits—something they can't change?

2. When people give you feedback on your performance, what do you hear? What do you say to yourself? Do you say 'I can get better next time, if I engage in focused effort to learn from my mistakes?' Or do you just give up, and say to yourself that you're no good?
3. Think of a skill you don't have, but might like to have. *What comes to mind?* Are the thoughts from a fixed mind-set (*'I'm not arty, so I'm not doing that'*) or a growth mind-set (*'I can learn to try, if I try, and I will get better with practice'*)?
4. How might you change what you usually and characteristically to colleagues to help change their performance for the better?
5. How might you change what you usually and characteristically *to yourself* to help change your own performance for the better?
6. What lessons regarding mind-sets could have been usefully applied to Tom Spengler?
7. Test your mind-set online at http://mindsetonline.com/testyourmindset/step1.php

Further Reading

Alderson-Day B, Weis S, McCarthy-Jones S, Moseley P, Smailes D, Fernyhough C. (2016) The brain's conversation with itself: Neural substrates of dialogic inner speech. Soc Cogn Affect Neurosci, 11:110–120.

Andrieux M, Proteau L. (2016). Observational learning: Tell beginners what they are about to watch and they will learn better. Front. Psychol., http://journal.frontiersin.org/article/10.3389/fpsyg.2016.00051/full.

Blackwell L, Trzesniewski K, Dweck CS (2007) Implicit theories of intelligence predict achievement across an adolescent transition: A longitudinal study and an intervention. Child Dev., 78:246–263.

Cimpian A, Arce HM, Markman EM, Dweck CS (2007) Subtle linguistic cues affect children's motivation. Psychol Sci., 18:314–326.

Dweck CS (2007) Mindset: The new psychology of success. Ballantine Books. (See also: The power of believing that you can improve https://www.ted.com/talks/carol_dweck_the_power_of_believing_that_you_can_improve?language=en)

Fernyhough C (2016) The voices within: The history and science of how we talk to ourselves. Profile Books, London.

Holtmaat A, Caroni P (2016) Functional and structural underpinnings of neuronal assembly formation in learning. Nat. Neurosci., 19:1553–1562. doi: 10.1038/nn.4418.

McCarthy-Jones, S and Fernyhough, C (2011) The varieties of inner speech. Consciousness and cognition, 20: 1586–1593.

O'Mara S, (2015) Why torture doesn't work: The neuroscience of interrogation. Harvard University Press, Cambridge, MA.

Paunesku D, Walton GM, Romero C, Smith EN, Yeager DS, Dweck CS (2015) Mind-set interventions are a scalable treatment for academic underachievement. Psychol Sci., 26(784–793). doi: 10.1177/0956797615571017.

Rattan A, Savani K, Chugh D, Dweck CS (2015) Leveraging mindsets to promote academic achievement: Policy recommendations. Perspect Psychol Sci, 10:721–726. doi: 10.1177/1745691615599383.

Schroder HS, Moran TP, Brent Donnellan M, Moser JS (2014) Mindset induction effects on cognitive control: A neurobehavioral investigation. Biol. Psychol., 103:27–37. http://dx.doi.org/10.1016/j.biopsycho.2014.08.004.

Vine SJ, Uiga L, Lavric A, Moore LJ, Tsaneva-Atanasova K, Wilson MR (2015) Individual reactions to stress predict performance during a critical aviation incident. Anxiety Stress Coping., 28:467–477. doi: http://dx.doi.org/10.1080/10615806.2014.986722.

4

Self-Regulation and Self-Control

This chapter focuses on neural and behavioural mechanisms involved in the regulation of our behaviour over time and how we can exert self-control in of different contexts.

> *The greatest weapon against stress is our ability to choose one thought over another.*
> —William James

Do You Control Yourself?

Let's start with a simple dichotomy. Who's in charge of you? Your conscious self or your non-conscious self? The answer seems obvious—it's our conscious self. However, a moment's reflection should show that this conclusion is not necessarily correct. Your conscious self spends almost no time during the course of the day attending to your breathing, attending to your heart rate, commanding your gut to digest food or worrying about the central pattern generators in the spinal cord that allow you to walk. If I ask you questions like: '*What colour is your car?*' '*How many bedrooms does your home have?*' '*What's your favourite food?*' the answers to these and a myriad other questions come crowding into consciousness quickly and effortlessly. They weren't in your consciousness just before I asked those questions, and yet they are now immediately accessible to consciousness. Where were they just before? The answer is that we have a very elaborate and extremely efficient set

© The Author(s) 2018
S. O'Mara, *A Brain for Business – A Brain for Life*, The Neuroscience of Business, https://doi.org/10.1007/978-3-319-49154-7_4

of cognitive and neural mechanisms that deliver to consciousness answers that are posed to us in our daily lives.

These remarkable cognitive and neural mechanisms can be challenged in all sorts of ways and are rarely bereft of an answer. If I say to you 'Do not think of a big large red elephant', immediately that big red large elephant will have come to mind, and you will have discovered that directed suppression of your own thoughts is extremely difficult. This is sometimes called 'ironic processing', because the entry into consciousness of the to-be-suppressed thought is automatic—showing how little control you can have over the contents of consciousness (Wegner and Schneider 2003; they chose not 'thinking about a white bear' as their example—see, it's happened again!). We don't need, for present purposes, to belabour or explore why it is that we are conscious. What is worth emphasising is the important fact that you are conscious and that just because a solution to a problem that you are dealing with is pushed into consciousness when you consider a problem space doesn't mean that you actually have to accept that solution. In other words, thoughts that intrude in consciousness are just that: they are thoughts that intrude in consciousness, and they are not part of your personal identity, necessarily. You can let them go or you can use this intrusion to generate further thoughts that might get you to better solution to a difficult and ill-defined problem.

Can You Choose Your Own Movements?

There seems nothing simpler than our capacity to engage in voluntary behaviour. You see the cup; you pick the cup up. You see the pen; you pick the pen up. You point to things; you choose not to point to things. You are, it seems, in control of your own body. So sit down, if you are not already sitting, and do the following test. Take your right hand, extend your index finger and make a figure 6 in the air. Very straightforward. Now, make a clockwise motion with your right foot. There: you've engaged in two simple self-chosen (albeit prompted) motor behaviours. Now do them together: the number 6 and the clockwise rotation of your foot. Watch what happens to your foot. Despite the fact that you've given the motor command to rotate your foot clockwise, you find your foot actually does something other than that you commanded! In other words, this exercise shows that actually the *'conscious commanding you'* is not necessarily in control of your own movements and that when it comes to a competition in the brain between your hands and your feet, your hands will most usually win. There are lots of reasons for this, and a very simple one is the fact that the brain cares much more about your hand and what it does than it does about your feet, because your hands, as a prehensile primate, are vitally important to all sorts of aspects of your behaviour. So, answer the question. Who's in charge of your movements? The 'you' that choses to move your finger in one direction, or the other 'you' that moved your foot in a direction that you didn't consciously choose?

Can You Control Your Own Reflexes?

We're all aware of our reflexes. If you touch something that's too hot, you withdraw your hand quickly and automatically, and your hand moves faster than you can think about it. The sensation of pain and the awareness that your hand has moved occur after the hand movement itself. This is because a simple 'reflex arc' from the hand, through the spinal cord and back out to the hand again controls a movement like this. If you have visited the doctor, at some point it is likely that the doctor will have conducted a simple test of reflexes in your legs. This is the tap below the knee to induce what's known as the 'patellar reflex', where your leg jerks up, and not under voluntary control. Most people would agree that we have little control over our reflexes. These are automatic, non-conscious, and they're clearly designed to serve adaptive purposes, where our behaviour is concerned: to not get burned, to move quickly and the like. Can you therefore consciously modify a reflex? It turns out that it is possible. Try the following test. Take your right index finger (having washed your hands). Extend your right index finger, and then open your mouth and carefully put your finger into your mouth to the point where you feel the 'gag reflex', that is the sensation of wanting to throw up, or of wanting to vomit. The gag reflex is a very important reflex. It has evolved to stop us choking or swallowing food items that are too large. It is known as an 'aerodigestive reflex', and pretty much everybody, at some point or another, will have experienced vomiting, and will have experienced a gag when they've swallowed something unpleasant that goes down the wrong way. Now the question is, can you modify this reflex? The answer is yes. Try the following. Take your left hand, open it, place your thumb across the palm of your hand and squeeze it until it hurts—not much, but it must hurt a little. Now just place that hand down to the side, all the while keeping the pressure up. Next, repeat the experiment we conducted before. Extend your right index finger and put it carefully into your mouth. What you will find is that your gag reflex has almost certainly disappeared. This is quite remarkable, isn't it? You've taken a reflex that is vital for survival, which plays an immediate adaptive function, and with a simple voluntary intervention, you can abolish it.

So, Who is in Charge of You?

The straightforward lessons to draw from these simple demonstrations are that we (our conscious selves) are not necessarily in control of our voluntary movements, and that we can, under some circumstances, control our own (nonconscious) reflex behaviours. More broadly, the lesson here should be obvious: that with the right knowledge and understanding, we can intervene in the functioning of our brains in ways that we would not necessarily have been able to predict at the outset.

Self-Control

Self-control is an especially important concept with profound implications for how we conduct and live our lives. At its simplest, self-control is the idea that we can defer gratification (in other words, postpone an immediate reward) in favour of a larger reward at a later time point. Children and animals are typically poor at self-control. It is a capacity that in the average individual gets better as you get older, principally in lockstep with the development of the frontal lobes. People with frontal lobe damage typically (but not always) have problems with self-control. This can manifest itself in a variety of ways, from an incapacity to control emotions, to an inability to suppress or moderate unwanted thoughts, to being unable to control impulses related to food, gambling, risk, sexual behaviour or a wide variety of other possibilities. The famous 'marshmallow experiments' provide a canonical example of how self-control manifests itself (Mischel 2014). In these experiments, young children are brought to the laboratory and they are offered a choice: an immediate reward consisting of one marshmallow, or if they are able to resist eating the marshmallow, two marshmallows at some future point in time. Remarkably, this simple experiment, involving the exertion of self-control over the consumption of a piece of confectionery, predicts a wide variety of life outcomes, even decades later.

Happily, we now know that the ability to delay gratification (in other words, to engage in self-control) is an acquirable skill. Its presence in the first place is profoundly affected by life experience: there may well be some heritable component as well. It should be emphasised, though, that particular and specific cognitive strategies demonstrate that self-control can be learned and can be enhanced throughout the life course. Returning to the marshmallow experiments, on longer-term follow-up, children who were capable of waiting for the deferred larger award had higher scholastic aptitude test scores as well as better social and cognitive functioning throughout adolescence. By the late 20s or early 30s, a variety of other positive indicators also appeared. Those who were able to wait the longest at the age of four were less overweight, had a better sense of their own self-worth, coped well with stress and frustration, and generally were able to pursue their life goals with greater effect. By their mid-40s, distinctive brain scan differences were seen between those who were effective delayers at the age of four or five compared to those who were not (Casey and colleagues 2011). There were important differences seen in brain regions that are involved in drug addiction and obesity. We can conclude that self-control is very important for being able to pursue long-term goals. In a financial context, humans are able to show remarkable levels of long-term planning under certain circumstances. It is not uncommon for humans to start pension planning in their 20s, in anticipation of deferred reward (namely a decent pension) in their late 60s or early 70s, a delay of consumption of several decades. This form of long-term, deferred gratification is found across generations—there are multi-generation mortgages and government bonds with maturity dates of 100 years or more. Self-control is also a vital part of everyday social life. People with poor impulse control, who grab every reward available to them at that moment, tend to have poor social and familial relations and will find great difficulty in building the forms of close, mutually supportive relationships required for success in family life and in organisational life.

Socioeconomic Status and Self-Control

There have been many studies focused on the issue of financial security, socioeconomic status and control at work. The famous Whitehall studies of civil servants in the United Kingdom government show, when you control other variables, that the lower your grade, the worse is your health status, relatively speaking (Marmot and colleagues 1991; Whitehall II). This reflects the fact that people who are higher in grade in the civil service tend to have a greater degree of control over their everyday work. Similarly, where people tend to have higher levels of control at work, they tend to have lower levels of blood pressure and vice versa. A general rule of thumb is that the lower one's income is, the lower is one's sense of control over oneself and one's environment, and the worse is one's health status (Lachman and Weaver 1998). The poor tend, on average, to die younger than the rich at all age categories across all countries.

Recent theorising, as has already been hinted at, suggests that self-control is an acquirable skill. This suggests that in certain respects the exercise of self-control is like the exercise of a muscle, that repetitively exercising it should, on the one hand, build the strength of self-control, but on the other hand suggests that it might lead, transiently, at least, to some level of loss of self-control because, like a muscle, it can only be taxed so far without a recovery period. The psychologist Roy Baumeister has suggested in particular that thinking of self-control as functioning like a muscle, which is strengthened through exercise but which tires as a result of that self-same exercise, is a useful metaphor (see Tierney and Baumeister 2011 for a full account). In what is now a classic experiment, Baumeister and his colleagues demonstrated that when you exert a lot of self-control in one situation, you might have less self-control in another. In this experiment, undergraduates are brought to the laboratory, which, cruelly, is set up with freshly baked chocolate chip cookies (which of course smell very tempting) and also slightly less palatable radishes. The undergraduates are then told that they could either eat the radishes or the chocolate chip cookies, but not both: they were not allowed to choose which ones they preferred. They were then given a series of very difficult or impossible to solve puzzle tasks. The experimenters found that, on average, those who had been given the freshly baked cookies and therefore did not have to exert self-control against temptation spent about twice as long on average attempting to solve the puzzles and attempted about twice as many puzzles on average compared to either a group that were given the radishes or a group that acted as a control who were not given any food at all. The key idea here is that making lots of choices can deplete willpower (the phenomenon of 'ego depletion'). President Barack Obama gave a famous example of this, where he stated 'You'll see I wear only gray or blue suits', [Obama] said. 'I'm trying to pare down decisions. I don't want to make decisions about what I'm eating or wearing. Because I have too many other decisions to make' (Baer 2014).

There has been a ferment of experimentation and controversy in the literature regarding the phenomenon of ego depletion, but some conclusions are reasonably safe to draw. First of all, sustained cognitive control is tiring (as we have already seen in the study regarding judges and their decisions). Second, optimal functioning of the brain is maintained by lots of regular and good quality sleep, regular aerobic exercise and time on as well as time off the task (this amounts to no more than the truism that regular breaks are a good thing when performing cognitively demanding tasks). Third, people's beliefs about the level of willpower that they have also impact on task performance. Those individuals who believe that their willpower is effectively unlimited show greater levels of perseverance at difficult tasks compared to those who do not (Job and colleagues 2010). Finally, people's beliefs about their own free will vary according to how they feel. In a simple but elegant experiment, psychologists Michael Ent and Roy Baumeister (2014) show that the degree of desire to empty one's bladder directly impacts on how much free will an individual believes that they have. This is easily demonstrated by having participants in experiments drink a litre of water at either the start or the end of an hour of puzzle-solving and asking them to rate, at the start and the end of that hour, how free they believe their own wills are. Unsurprisingly, those with full bladders believe that they have much less free will compared to those with empty bladders. Beware long business meetings where there are plentiful supplies of coffee (which acts as a diuretic) and water where, for reasons of face-saving, toilet breaks are impossible and an urgent necessity to conclude a deal is present. You may find yourself unable to prevent an unfavourable deal in these circumstances!

Motivation and Money

Why do you work? Is it simply for the money? The answer is almost certainly not. Would you never work again if you won or inherited so much money that you would not need to work again? The answer for most people is no—they will work again, although they may take considerable time off and may cease their current employment quickly. Humans do respond to all manner of non-monetary and indeed non-monetisable incentives—including social incentives such as working within a cohesive team toward a commonly agreed goal. The value that individuals place on these other incentives is considerable and is deeply woven into the structure of our brains. Non-monetary incentives activate brain areas responsible for rewards and punishments as well as brain areas responsible for all manner of other feelings (such as warmth, cold, disgust) that affect our behaviour. Tom Spengler, our medium-cap-pharma chief in the prologue, was well paid; his motive in attempting the three-way merger was not principally to earn more money (although that may have been a happy consequence). Rather, Tom's motivation was to create a larger institutional entity that would long survive him—an institution within which he would become replaceable, but which would be an enduring legacy to his efforts. The mistake many economists have often made is to undervalue and under-price non-monetary incentives in human behaviour. The psychological value of non-monetary incentives is profound. Creating an enduring institution is Tom's goal—the money is secondary and merely facilitates what he is trying to do. After all, humans have been around much longer than money has been around; our modern financial system is just that—modern. It has been around for a comparatively short period of time—just a few hundred years in developed economies. Money as a medium of exchange is obviously important in directing, modifying and channelling behaviour productively, but it is not all-important.

Self-Control and the Individual

Self-control refers to our capacity to engage in behaviours that are required to attain our long-term goals and our ability to defer gratification. Self-control is essential for the normal conduct of social life. It is absolutely central to organisational life. In fact, it could be argued that organisational life is built upon a foundation of individual self-control, simply because organisations, be they businesses, armies or whatever, are constructed from an array of diverse individuals who must learn to work together despite their individual proclivities and differences. Children do not have full self-control, as self-control is a capacity that develops over time, in concert with brain development.

To demonstrate how self-control wavers, let us do the following simple thought experiment ourselves. Imagine I come to your office; it's just before lunch, and you're feeling a bit hungry. I offer you a choice as follows. You can have a bar of chocolate today, now (the indulgent option); or you can have an apple now (the virtuous option); or you can have the chocolate next week; or you can have the fruit next week. Experiments of this type show that on average, three-quarters of people will choose the fruit next week, and about 70 per cent of people will choose the chocolate today (Read and Van Leeuwen 1998). In other words, people show time-inconsistent preferences where self-control is concerned. We are very good at choosing good things for our future selves, but we are often not so good at choosing good things for our present self. A similar preference is shown where movie choices are concerned. If people are offered a choice between lowbrow or highbrow movies now, or lowbrow and highbrow movies for next week, people will typically choose a lowbrow film for now, and they will choose for their future self a highbrow movie next week (Read et al. 1999). In other words, people have a preference for choosing 'fun' now, on average, and deferring the 'good stuff' to next week. Self-control is exercised for our best future selves, but less so for our present selves. This is especially the case under circumstances where there are stresses and strains present, where one is hungry, where one is tired or there are multiple or competing demands on one's attention.

What Does Self-Control Consist of?

We can think of self-control as consisting essentially of four components. The first is self-regulation, the second is emotional regulation, the third is cognitive control, and the fourth is locus of control. The balance between these components leads to choices being made and behaviours being executed (whether this means taking a deep breath and exerting emotional self-control despite extreme provocation or letting go and shouting or bullying the person who happens to be at hand). Self-regulation refers to your ability to control your own behaviour according to the particular demands of the social context and social milieu that you are in. This may involve self-censorship; it may involve engaging in 'go along to get along' behaviours; or it may mean simply adopting the cultural norms and mores of the situation that you find yourself in. Emotional regulation is a slightly different concept. It involves monitoring your own emotional state, being able to evaluate it 'on the fly', and control, redirect or suppress an emotion, especially with regard to its intensity. Emotional regulation is central to preventing emotional outbursts, but equally is central to being able to regulate one's own mood. Cognitive control refers to how well one can manage, engage, focus or direct one's own cognitive processes so that they are focused on problem-solving or whatever the needs of the moment happen to be and to be able to do so despite the presence of distractions. The final component of self-control is one that is not often considered to be part of self-control, but really is a part of it: this is the extent to which you believe your behaviour allows you to exert control over your life. In other words, your 'locus of control'. Locus of control turns out to be an extremely important variable, especially where stress and performance at work are concerned. It refers to the idea or the belief that you have over the extent to which you can control outcomes in your own life. It also refers to your ability to handle or cope with the diverse challenges, demands and strains that life in general, or people in particular, may pose for you. There are marked differences in the extent to which people answer questions such as the following: (1) success is pretty much determined by forces outside of our control; (2) what happens in my life is determined by forces outside of my control. One especially useful method for training self-control in a work context is 'simulation'. There are lots of situations where self-control might fail. Think of a golfer choking while making a crucial putt; think of a stage actor 'corpsing' on stage; or think of a manager tasked with making a crucial financial decision to meet a quarterly target where their job might be on the line. In all of these cases, tiredness, stress, exhaustion and lack of training can, and most likely will, impact terribly on subsequent performance. There are ways of dealing with these problems. One powerful method is 'simulation'. Simulation, or to give it another name, rehearsal, involves listing ahead of time the likely issues and triggers that may cause problems and the potential solutions for those problems. The explicit purpose of simulation in this context is to ensure that a tired, stressed, hungry worker does not resort to sudden impulsive, rapid cognitive and behavioural shortcuts that may in turn prove to be disastrous subsequently.

Self-Regulation and Self-Talk

In the discussion on self-regulation, to this point we've given comparatively little emphasis to the role of self-talk. Self-talk has a very important role in self-regulation because it allows you to plan what you want to do before you actually do it. However, self-talk can impose a cognitive load. Easily remembering your intentions and plans and executing them imposes a cognitive load, and keeping the implementation intentions in a form that allows you to execute them easily can become problematic. There are a number of ways to deal with this. One is to adopt checklists. The other is to decrease the load by designing the environment to allow you to avoid the problem behaviour in the first place. In other words, to achieve particular goals, a smart way to avoid depleting or at least taxing willpower, and avoiding cognitive fatigue, is to attempt to design the environment to avoid temptation in the first place. If you have a problem with late evening snacking, then simply do not buy the snacks and store them in the cupboard.

Instead, buy fruits and use these to snack on instead—a simple way to cut out the temptation posed by chocolate and crisps. A neat experiment by Marina Milyauskaya and Michael Inzlicht (in press) explores just this strategy. They use, initially, the experience sampling method described in Chapter 2, where they had their participants use smartphones that pinged them with messages on a several-times-a-day basis, they kept diaries, and so on. At the start of the study the students had to state four goals that they wished to attain over the coming period of time. They found an important and interesting result, one that goes contrary to much popular thinking. Exercising self-control on a frequent basis did not lead to goal attainment, whereas experiencing a decreased number of temptations from the environment did lead to goal attainment. They suggest that experiencing temptations and then attempting to resist them can be exhausting. So the simpler strategy is to avoid them completely in the first place. This is a much simpler and much less cognitively demanding and exhausting tactic.

For a checklist to work, Gawande and others suggest that they need to be direct and to the point; they need to be simple; they should provide particular reminders of critical steps and especially key steps that are most often missed; finally, they should be quick to complete. Of course, checklists can be cheated. A checklist, if it is not implemented appropriately, can be ignored. A checklist in and of itself can't make people use it, and there will be situations that the checklist simply does not speak to. They do not substitute for a brain. Instead, a checklist is designed to assist or supplement a tired and overworked set of frontal lobes to ensure that they get the appropriate supports from the environment to arrive at the best possible outcome.

Self-Regulation and Self-Control

Ibrahim Senay and colleagues (2010) show that, in certain cases, self-talk can have an important effect on task completion. Participants were given anagrams to solve and they were divided into two groups. One group were simply prompted beforehand to ask themselves 'whether they would do the task', and a second group were prompted to resolve to themselves that they would complete this task. Group 1, who asked themselves whether or not they would complete the task, outperformed Group 2. So the implication here is that a question prompting us whether or not you will do something is more effective as a goad to completing an action than simply engaging in a resolution. They went on then and explored this effect in two further groups. They compared individuals who wrote down the simple phrase 'Will I do this?' to another group who wrote down 'I will do this.' The 'Will I' group outperformed the 'I will' group. The lesson they draw is that focusing on the outcome is less effective than focusing on how to achieve the outcome and that asking questions mobilises non-conscious processing resources that lead to answers that allow you to attain a goal, whereas simply stating your intention or making a resolution does not translate into goal attainment, irrespective of how strongly or firmly that resolution is made to oneself.

Thinking About the Future

A very important aspect of self-regulation and self-control is an orientation to the future, deferring gratification from the here and now to achieve some goal in the future. One method that people have attempted widely to use is to engage in so-called 'positive thinking'. Gabriel Oettingen (2014), a psychologist at New York University, has, in an important series of experimental studies, focused on the power of 'positive thinking'. Her headline conclusion is an important one: there is no power to positive thinking *per se*. Engaging in positive thinking, indulging in fantasies about the future, engaging in extended daydreaming in the hope that the goal will be attained, leads to more negative outcomes than not engaging in positive fantasies about the future to begin with. She shows, for example, that students at a university who have a crush on another student are much less likely to do anything about that crush, the more they indulge they indulge in wish-fulfilling fantasies about attaining a relationship with that crush, compared to students who actually go and do something about it. In other words, engaging in a future-oriented positive fantasy acts as a brake or a block, where attaining the desired-for outcome is concerned. Oettingen's reasonable hypothesis suggests that indulging in or engaging in extensive positive thinking takes away from the mental effort that is required to achieve a goal. In other words, focusing on the outcome takes away from figuring out the actual concrete steps that are needed for action. She further suggests that positive thinking leads to a feeling of having achieved one's goals despite not having achieved the goal. This she refers to as 'mental attainment'. More remarkably, her work suggests also that there is a link between engaging in active fantasies about goals and subsequent bouts of mild depression. The key point here is that self-talk, in terms of behavioural regulation, can be both positive and negative and that self-talk that leads to excessive rumination can lead to dysphoria, or feeling bad about oneself, whereas self-talk and rumination that links to concrete actions, to steps that allow one to attain a goal, are much more important and much less likely to lead to depression.

Oettingen also argues that achieving the goal in your mind via fantasising or daydreaming leads to feelings of attainment of that goal. It feels good in the moment, but fundamentally distracts from the steps that are needed to achieve that goal. In other work, she and her collaborators have found that in schoolchildren, fantasies about exemplary examination performance are correlated with poor examination outcomes and a greater incidence of dysphoria. The key here is that excessive dreaming about the future leads to, eventually, a gloomier, darker mood—a mild dysphoric state that colours what otherwise would be a positive mood. So advice focused on positive thinking is entirely misplaced. It may lead to pleasant feelings in the here and now, but it will lead to gloomier feelings in the future and it will act as a block to action. This is not to say that positive thinking is all bad. What is needed is to couple positive thinking about the end state—the wonderful goal to be achieved—with the actual steps that are needed to attain that goal. Thinking in this way causes one to focus on whether or not the goal is realistic or attainable to begin with. If it is not, if there are no concrete steps that can be taken in the real world to attain the goal, well then the goal can be removed or dismissed from consciousness or from strategic planning at the organisational level. In fact, it is this kind of fantasy-oriented thinking that bedevils so many strategic plans in business. Business leaders attempt to attain major visions, and the vision itself, of course, is one of 'sunny uplands' of great progress and great success. The missing piece is the series of concrete steps to work toward that goal. A useful exercise, then, is when a goal has been stated in clear terms to engage in a forward-looking set of concrete steps that allow one to attain that goal. In other words, the concrete sequence of changes that are required to allow the goal to occur and to work backwards from the goal to where you are now. These exercises should be undertaken by independent groups and the job of the leader really should be one of ensuring that the groups do their job in a cohesive fashion. A comparison between these forward-looking and backward-looking action-takings should allow one to discover whether or not the goal is realistic and can be attained or not.

Behavioural Change Through Rescripting

Timothy Wilson (2011), in his important book, '*Redirect*', suggests that there are really three ways we can engage in behavioural change, focusing on our self-narratives. One is to engage in '*story editing*'. The second is to engage in '*story prompting'*, and the third is *'do good be good'*. *Story editing* involves focusing on how we talk to ourselves about ourselves and our social world, and to change our story what we need to do is to write it down, or write down some aspect of the behaviour that we would like to change. Wilson suggests that we should do this on several occasions, certainly at least three times over three nights, and preferably four. Doing this allows you to impose your own narrative on your problems. And, of course, sleep turns out to be a very important collaborator in arriving at solutions to your problems. *Story prompting* involves not simply writing your narrative as in story editing, but choosing in the course of your writing paths or prompts that focus on how behavioural change is possible in a particular and desired direction. *Do good be good* is an approach that has been demonstrated many times to work. This is where you simply change the behaviour first and changing your behaviour in turn allows you to change the cycle of self-talk and self-thought. So you're nervous as a public speaker? Well, go and do public speaking. You'll hate it, but you'll gradually master it, and what you say to yourself about it will change as a result of having engaged in it. The writing exercise where you take something that is an irritation or a difficulty or a problem originated with the psychologist James Pennebaker (1997), and it now known as the Pennebaker Writing Exercise. In the simple act of doing this writing exercise three times for 15 minutes demonstrably improves how people feel about themselves. The other major advantage of these writing and rescripting exercises is that they encourage a 'perspective taking' approach, by allowing you to engage in mental time travel, where you can go backwards in time, watch what has happened; go forwards in time, see how it plays out; to the present, and go further forwards in time again and see what the possible consequences might be. This distance-taking, where you observe what has happened from the outside by means of the imposed writing exercise, allows you to explore a variety of ways that you might feel about a particular situation. Going back and revisiting it and then travelling forward from it may give you a greater sense of self-control and mastery over the situation, for example.

Exercises

1. Think about when you last succumbed to a temptation, despite your best efforts. Now, list the factors that you can number that prompted it; list things present in your environment prior to the temptation occurring; and

list your feeling before, during, and after the temptation, to the very best extent that you can. What have you learned from this exercise?

2. Think about when you last successfully resisted temptation, despite intense provocation. Now, list the factors that you can remember that prompted you to resist temptation; list the factors present in the environment prior to the temptation; list your feelings before, during and after successfully resisting the temptation. What have you learned from this?

3. List, using short words or phrases, three things that you find difficult to resist.

4. List, using short words or phrases, three things that you find easy to resist.

5. Thinking about no. 4, things that you find easy to resist, consider the ways that you engage in self-talk that allows you to resist the temptation and exert self-control in a stressful situation. Do the same exercise regarding your self-talk for those moments when you find it difficult to resist temptation.

6. What are the things Tom Spengler finds difficult to resist? Would have resisting them been in any way useful to him?

Further Reading

Baer D (2014) Always wear the same suit: Obama's presidential productivity secrets. Fast company; https://www.fastcompany.com/3026265/work-smart/always-wear-the-same-suit-obamas-presidential-productivity-secrets

Casey BJ, Somerville LH, Gotlib IH, Ayduk O, Franklin NT, Askren MK, Jonides J, Berman MG, Wilson NL, Teslovich T, Glover G, Zayas V, Mischel W, Shoda Y (2011) Behavioral and neural correlates of delay of gratification 40 years later. Proc. Natl. Acad. Sci., 108:14998–15003. doi: 10.1073/pnas.1108561108.

Ent MR, Baumeister RF (2014) Embodied free will beliefs: Some effects of physical states on metaphysical opinions. Conscious Cogn., 27:147–154. doi: http://dx.doi.org/10.1016/j.concog.2014.05.001.

Job V, Dweck CS, Walton GM (2010) Ego depletion—is it all in your head?: Implicit theories about willpower affect self-regulation. Psychol. Sci., 21:1686–1693. doi: 10.1177/0956797610384745.

Lachman ME, Weaver SL (1998) The sense of control as a moderator of social class differences in health and well-being. J Pers Soc Psychol., 74(763–773). doi: http://dx.doi.org/10.1037/0022-3514.74.3.763.

Marmot MG, Davey Smith G, Stansfield S, Patel C, North F, Head J, White I, Brunner E, Feeney A (1991) Health inequalities among British civil servants: The

Whitehall II study. Lancet, 337(8754): 1387–1393. doi: 10.1016/0140-6736 (91)93068-K.

Milyavskaya M, Inzlicht M (in press) What's so great about self-control? Examining the importance of effortful self-control and temptation in predicting real-life depletion and goal attainment. Soc. Psychol. Person. Sci., https://static1.square space.com/static/550b09eae4b0147d03eda40d/t/5804d4a820099e2af777ce7f/ 1476711593305/whats-so-great-about-self-control.pdf.

Mischel W (2014) The marshmallow test: Mastering self-control. Little, Brown, New York.

Oettingen G (2014) Rethinking positive thinking: Inside the new science of motivation. Penguin Random House, New York, NY.

Pennebaker JW (1997) Writing about emotional experiences as a therapeutic process. Psychol Sci., 8: 162–166. doi: 10.1111/j.1467-9280.1997.tb00403.x.

Read D, Loewenstein G, Kalyanaraman S (1999) Mixing virtue and vice: combining the immediacy effect and the diversification heuristic. J. Behav. Decis. Making, 12:257–273. http://online.wsj.com/public/resources/documents/ ReadLoewenstein_VirtueVice_JBDM99.pdf. doi: 10.1002/(SICI)1099-0771 (199912)12:4<257::AID-BDM327>3.0.CO;2-6;.

Read D, Van Leeuwen B (1998) Predicting hunger: The effects of appetite and delay on choice. *Organ Behav Hum Decis Process*, 76:189–205.

Senay I, Albarracín D, Noguchi K (2010) Motivating goal-directed behavior through introspective self-talk: The role of the interrogative form of simple future tense. Psychol Sci., 21(499–504). doi: 10.1177/0956797610364751.

Tierney J, Baumeister RF. (2011) Willpower: Rediscovering the greatest human strength. Penguin Press, New York.

Wegner DM, Schneider DJ (2003) The white bear story. Psychol Inq., 14: 326–329.

Whitehall II (the *Stress and Health* Study) http://www.ucl.ac.uk/whitehallII/

Wilson TD (2011) Redirect: The surprising new science of psychological change. Little, Brown, New York.

5

The Importance of Cognitive Biases

This chapter explores how it is that we make reliable and systematic errors in our thinking and how these systematic biases can affect the decisions that we make.

> 'The general root of superstition is that men observe when things hit, and not when they miss; and commit to memory the one, and forget and pass over the other'.
> (Francis Bacon, 1561–1626, English philosopher of science)

Decision-making by humans is biased in a variety of ways. Humans are often very poor decision-makers, failing to take account of important information that can be critically important for decision-making and action. Francis Bacon, in the quote above, gives one very good example—humans are good at taking account of hits, but are poor at remembering misses. Hence, the huge number of superstitious beliefs about 'signs' that predict the weather, or the stock market, or whatever. Departures from what might be expected on the basis of a purely rational calculation following the rules of logic and what economists refer to as 'utility maximisation' are pervasive features of human thinking. It is also starting to become clear that these biases serve outcomes that are other than a straightforward utility or reward-maximising function for individuals. Biases in decision-making may serve to reinforce affiliation or strength of the bonds within a tightly defined group, for example. Biases may also serve to punish behaviour that is seen to be transgressive—taking too much reward for too little effort (free-loading), for instance. In this case, there may even be a willingness to engage in *costly punishment*—to punish a member of one's own group, or to punish an opposing group, even if there is an economic cost to oneself and to one's

© The Author(s) 2018
S. O'Mara, *A Brain for Business – A Brain for Life*, The Neuroscience of Business, https://doi.org/10.1007/978-3-319-49154-7_5

group (Heinrich and colleagues 2006). The question posed by the group is simple: 'what sort of a hit are we willing to take in order to teach the other lot a lesson?' Both history and experiments show that humans are willing to take punishments in order to teach the other side a lesson—costly punishments that would not be prescribed by a purely rational calculus. The other side in the dispute may assume that there will be no costly punishment, as in believing that 'they won't impose trade sanctions on us. After all, they sell us a lot of cheese (or cars, or wine, or shoes—or whatever)'. But they can, and they will. A refusal to recognise in a negotiation that one side will act contrary to their own narrowly defined economic self-interest to ensure a broader political, legal and social lesson is learned is a very common mistake.

Cognitive biases are a pervasive and universal aspect of human thinking. In essence, they are systematic biases in gathering information and in thinking that lead to a deviation from rationality calculations or even simply what is demonstrably 'good and fair judgement'. The case study in the Chapter 1 of this book provides many examples of many cognitive biases, and we will discuss a few them below. There are huge numbers of biases—the Wikipedia entry for '*Cognitive Bias*' lists more than 175 of them. The famous cognitive scientist, Daniel Kahneman, was awarded the 2002 Nobel Memorial Prize in Economic Sciences, his citation reading that his award was '*for having integrated insights from psychological research into economic science, especially concerning human judgment and decision-making under uncertainty*' 2011. His book '*Thinking, Fast and Slow*' (2011) explores many cognitive biases, many of which he discovered and explored experimentally; it is important reading to supplement this chapter. We are aware of many of these cognitive predilections already. Phrases such as 'wishful thinking' or 'cherry-picking' reflect the idea that when we think about a topic, or argue in favour of a particular point of view, that our thinking is in some way biased. We are engaging in a form of argument where our thinking doesn't fairly, reliably and accurately reflect reality or the truth. Instead, we are choosing evidence to suit our wishes and beliefs rather than actually reflecting reality as best we can.

There are many examples of this kind of thinking in the real world. Politics in particular is bedevilled by this. People who identify with a political candidate will deny data or evidence that is contrary to their point of view—in other words, the evidence is retrofitted to one's point of view rather than adjusting one's point of view to the data. A wonderful and egregious example of this arises with respect to political polling for elections. In the 2011 campaign for the Presidency of the United States, the political poll aggregators consistently showed that Barack Obama was reliably leading the Republican nominee, Mitt Romney, to the chagrin and disbelief of (many of) Romney's supporters.

They alleged, without meaningful statistical sampling evidence, that the polls were skewed. Thus, the 'unskewing' industry was born: Dean Chambers, a Romney supporter, was convinced that the polls were skewed in some way (search for 'unskew polls 2012 dean chambers'). The reality of the polling was that the burden of support in the election was against Chambers' preferred candidate, and an honest analysis of the polls would have told you that ahead of time. An honest and veridical analysis, though, comes with a price: acknowledging that your preferred candidate is doing badly at the polls. It's much easier to spend time 'unskewing' polling data than getting out the vote for your candidate. You might actually have to go out in the cold and rain to try and convince uninterested voters on their doorsteps! Of course, polling is a complex technical affair, involving issues to do with sample size, confidence intervals, sampling demographics and a whole host of other variables. In the US example, sites like the Princeton Election Consortium (run by the neuroscientist and data analyst, Sam Wang) or 538.com give a sense of the technicalities involved and therefore how individual judgement can go so terribly wrong. Furthermore, the memory that people have for what the polls showed, and what they actually showed, can be very faulty indeed. And, occasionally, pollsters do get things wrong when they make modelling assumptions about the relationship between their polling and the underlying trend in reality. And some will do a better job of it than others. Where biases become maladaptive is precisely in these cases: information gathering can be conducted over an extended period of time, and the deliberative processes associated with the information gathered can also be conducted over a prolonged period of time. The key point of course is having time—more good data are better than less bad data, all things being equal, assuming of course that decision-making is being driven empirically—i.e., that it reflects the reality of the world as it is rather than as one might like it to be. While the singular Steve Jobs may have been able to deploy a 'reality distortion field' to get his way in business, and to impose his very particular vision on business, he also had many failures (the Apple III, the Lisa, the hockey puck mouse, NEXT, Apple TV…). Even he could not distort reality so much that it would conform to his vision of what it should or could be.

Thinking about Cognitive Biases

The sheer number of cognitive biases that have been identified (175 or more; Kahneman 2011; Nesbitt 2015), and the overlap between at least some of them, is itself a major problem. This statement alone should convince you of their reality: humans have a limited capacity to process information arising from the world beyond the brain, to combine this knowledge with prior knowledge they already have stored in their brains, and a limited capacity process this information quickly and efficiently in order to serve the adaptive needs of the present. This is where one type of bias may arise—from our limited capacity to process the necessary information to make a decision. The effect is one that results in our brains doing a 'good enough' job, most of the time, than a perfect job all the time. After all, if I mistake that moving shape at the edge of my vision for a tiger—even though it is actually a stippled bush, moving in the wind—little harm is done if I run away or adopt a defensive posture on the basis of a rapid decision made with imperfect information. On the other hand, if it is a tiger, and it is hungry, well then I am done for, if I take too long to make a decision about just what that ambiguous moving shape is, just because I need more information to identify the tiger with certainty!

The huge number of identified cognitive biases has led to a variety of classification schemes to help make them easier to understand, and thence to identify, and where possible, to work around. One especially useful scheme has recently be elaborated by Buster Benson (2017), who has classified cognitive biases along four, straightforward, problems that our cognitive biases help us to solve. Biases, as Benson reminds us, can be adaptive because they solve quickly and efficiently problems arising from 'information overload, lack of meaning, the need to act fast, and how to know what needs to be remembered for later'. A 'quick and dirty' solution that solves the problem of the 'now' is the one that will be used. The problems that biases can shortcut can be grouped as follows:

1. ***Too much information:*** there is too much information in the world. You have select, and select quickly, in order to decide, in order to act. What do you select? Why? You are a CEO and your major country units have seen a sudden collapse in sales. You have lots of fine-grained information from point of sale terminals and from your warehouses. More information that you know what do with: sales per employee, sales per region, sales by market sector, sales by sales force team; you have information on the cost of sales, regulations, non-tariff barriers, local tariffs. This is what happened to traditional camera makers; it is what happened to the sales of compact disks. It happens quickly and predictably when a previously patented drug goes off-label, and generic manufacturers move in. It has happened to taxis when companies like Uber move in.

2. ***Not enough meaning:*** often, the meaning of the information we have to hand is not obvious, because we don't have enough information, or the information is of poor quality, or has been collected in a biased fashion. What do you do? Why? You are a comic book producer, and your sales are

collapsing, and fast. People are moving away from newsprint. What does this mean? Does it mean you become a digital comic book producer? Will that save you? If you were Marvel Comics, it meant that you were no longer a comic book producer. It meant that quickly you became a company in the entertainment business, with interests in movies and associated products, and you owned a whole universe of characters. This is your new business.

3. ***Need to act fast:*** sometimes, decisions must be taken quickly, and either problem 1 or 2 is present. You are a doctor, and the patient is bleeding out. You have lots of one type of information (there is blood, and lots of it), but little of any other information (Where is the blood coming from? Why isn't it clotting?). You are a CEO, and one of your major country units has seen a sudden collapse in sales. You haven't visited for a while. What's going on? Now, what should you do? Who's to blame? Someone? Maybe no one? Did technological changes render you redundant? Did you persist with attempting to sell horses for personal transport despite the advent of the motor car? Do you transform your business quickly from something you know intimately (grass-eating engines, i.e., horses) to something you know nothing about (internal combustion engines)?

4. ***What should we remember?*** Again, there is too much information, and much that we need to know, we can know offload to external cognitive devices like books or the internet, or indeed the brains of specialists in the area. We need therefore to select information, and we select based on what we already know and can readily hang new knowledge onto. Maybe the sales collapse has resulted because of non-tariff barriers that have stalled our product in some obscure customs warehouse in the middle of nowhere. We remember that happened once before selling into a new territory. Maybe that's what's happened. You chase the problem you remember a previous solution for, rather than trying to find out objectively what's actually happened. In the case of CD sales, a new digital infrastructure, combined with file sharing, initially sandbagged your business. An inability to adapt to music streaming services exacerbated the problem. And trying to shut them down will have as much likelihood of success as stagecoaches opposing the widespread adoption of the motor car.

Remember, there are many cognitive biases (we will name and explore some of them below)—and they may indeed be adaptive, depending on the problem you are trying to solve. Where the problem must be solved rapidly, with incomplete information and a high degree of ambiguity, decisions made and actions taken, biases will most likely be adaptive. Where the problem is ambiguous, the information gathering for it takes time, where there are extensive deliberative processes involved, and the outcomes are uncertain or arguable, cognitive biases are likely to be present, and they are likely to cause a deviation from an optimal course of action. This happens most often where the end has already been decided (usually for ideological reasons), and the evidence collected, and the strategy adopted, are retrofitted to ensure that the end chosen occurs. Of course, reality doesn't bend to our wishes or biases so easily, and disaster may await. Hence, the failure of 'unskewing': the polling data truly reflected the underlying reality.

Tom Spengler's Cognitive Biases in Action

The scenario offered in Chapter 1 is fictional, but it has elements recognisable from the history of corporate mergers and acquisitions, where companies do attempt friendly and occasionally hostile mergers, acquisitions and takeovers. Sometimes these mergers or acquisitions are very successful and create value; sometimes they are not and are disasters that destroy value. The scenario presented will be used here as a case study to illustrate some of the most important cognitive biases and how they distort the judgement of a supposedly hard-headed, numbers-oriented business person.

Tom saw what he thought was an opportunity, and then pushed hard for it, creating a team that did his bidding, and seemingly had won over his board, but hadn't, it seems, consulted his major shareholders who had a great deal of say in the outcome too. He also seemingly did not give a great deal of thought to his opposite numbers in the companies he was hoping to merge with. They obviously had thoughts of their own and a willingness to see them through. It seems Tom give very little time to thinking about the downsides of what he was proposing. He also pretty obviously was neglecting his own brain health, possibly to the detriment of his optimal cognitive functioning (by getting little sleep and aerobic exercise), which led him to use some mild stimulants (caffeine and nicotine). Heart health seems to have been a problem for him too—overweight, flushed face, smoking and eventually a heart attack.

Pre-Meeting Biases

Tom seems to have engaged in a combination of *confirmation bias* and the *focusing illusion*. Confirmation bias (sometimes called *myside bias*) occurs when you collect evidence or information that supports or confirms your own particular point of view and you discount information that is contrary to your point of view. As the novelist George Orwell put it in his famous political novel, *1984*, 'the best books…are those that tell you what you know already'. The *focusing illusion* is a cognitive bias that emphasises only upside arguments (local benefits), but ignores costs. Tom certainly seems to have considered only the positive aspects of the merger and has ignored the negative aspects of the merger. There are costs to the merger in time and money that should have given pause. More than this, Tom has assembled a team that seems deliberately to have been constructed so that they will do his bidding, and not oppose his wishes, or tell him unwelcome news. Tom has also constructed a financial case, using a biddable financial analyst, that entirely suits his own wishes, and which misprices the risks associated with the merger. Moreover, he is also trying to make good the costs associated with his previous failed attempt at a merger—the '*sunk cost*' fallacy. Economists emphasise that money spent and lost is just that—decisions should be made at the margin rather than trying to recover previously lost costs. These are gone, so forget about them: instead, concentrate on what is the correct thing to do now, in the light of what you now know, and forget past costs. An underlying problem with the sunk cost fallacy is the more general problem of '*loss aversion*'. Generally, we dislike losses much more than we like gains and therefore prefer try to make good losses. We won't sell shares that have lost value, preferring to hold on to them in the hope of them coming good. Crystallising the loss is itself unpleasant. Underlying changes in brain regions that compute losses and gains reflect decreases in brain regions that represent reward, among other things (see Tom and colleagues 2007).

Another problem that may occur is *groupthink*—a well-known and sometimes misunderstood idea. Groupthink is not the idea that a group of unconnected but demographically similar individuals happen to think the same thing. Groupthink occurs under very specific conditions: when a group makes poor decisions *because of high levels of within-group cohesion and a desire to minimise within-group conflict*. This might happen in an exhausted, embattled and worn-out Government Cabinet, but can and will just easily arise in the sort of group that Tom has assembled, supposedly to drive the merger, but which really exists to do his bidding. Working under some degree of duress (the threat of being replaced or fired) for a boss who appears to be something of a bully, and who is very certain of his own judgement, will be stressful and difficult, especially for those who wish to do a good job. Under these conditions, the necessary critical analysis simply does not occur. We have seen a different type of groupthink seize individual behaviour many times in financial and other markets. Recent examples are the contagion within financial institutions associated with the dotcom boom (and subsequent dotcom bust). A more recent example is the sudden acceleration and deceleration of property values throughout the western world caused in part by competition between financial institutions for what they uniformly misperceived as the capacity for property prices to move in an upwards direction only. Groupthink can be reduced by the group having an extensive network of weak ties to other individuals and groups. Weak ties can be informational ties: ties to others can provide us with novel ideas and knowledge and provide a route to a 'reality-test' planned courses of action. An extensive national and international weak tie network might provide information that would otherwise not be available. Another way to avoid groupthink is to deliberately design group deliberations to question, test and probe the conclusions of the group—this issue is discussed in detail in Chapter 6.

Another pervasive cognitive bias is known as '*identity protective cognition*' (Kahan 2007). We humans are members of social groups and social tribes. Our social groups and social tribes can be very rewarding and comforting and can come to represent very important aspects of our personal identities. Social scientists have often noted the exceptional strength of intra-group ties for social groups that are at best fringe in their relationship to what we know of the world scientifically. The moving target presented by the anti-vaccination community provides a fine example of a community impervious to reason and logic and, more particularly, to data. If you are a member of such a group and you are outraged by what I have just said, take a deep breath. Don't critique it. Think: are you engaging in identity-protective cognition? Are you refusing to entertain evidence in a particular way? Are you discounting the views of scientists merely because the group you are part of consists of lots of people who are opposed to vaccines because they are 'unnatural'? (Actually, nothing could be more natural than a vaccine, and nothing could be more unnatural than death in a car crash.) A truism of human behaviour is that people are incentive-driven (even by perverse incentives). Tom was paying his people well: it was in their short-term financial interests to go along with his plans. The American writer, Upton Sinclair, probably explains it best: 'It is difficult to get a man to understand something when his salary depends upon his not understanding it'. This will have affected Tom's team's thinking: the certainty of getting fired, and losing a salary, versus going along with his plans (which might have turned out well, after all).

Fundamental Attribution Error

Solely focusing on individuals and their behaviour and ignoring the situations within which their behaviour occurs is known as the fundamental attribution error. It is a cognitive bias caused by the salience of the person and the relative invisibility of the system (group norms, laws, rules, etc.). Criminals convicted of crimes will typically blame the situation ('I was provoked'), and observers will blame the person ('you didn't exercise self-control, despite provocation'). The lesson for organisations is simple: changing personnel is not enough to solve problems, because the dysfunctional system itself persists. We need substantial systemic changes too. In the case of political decisions, for example, these are often taken within a group context (think Cabinet collective responsibility), even though the policy itself might be strongly identified with a single individual, such as the responsible government minister. Behind the minister sits the invisible ministerial department, special advisors and others—but our bandwidth is limited, and it takes a special effort not to focus solely on the person, but also to try and see the system around them.

Perspective Taking

Marcus Aurelius, the Roman Emperor, famously said in his 'Meditations' that 'everything we see is a perspective, not the truth'. He was hinting at the idea that all we can do is sample some fraction of the information available to us in the environment and that we inevitably adopt a particular perspective when trying to understand things. This perspective may blind us to what others might be thinking. An important task in business and management is to try and understand and identify the motivations of others—to engage in 'perspective taking'. Perspective taking may occur during meetings or negotiations or even at a distance, where evidence to interpret the intentions of others may be scant or non-existent. In these cases, reasoning from one's own dispositions and biases and assuming that the other person or team will think and behave likewise is a common phenomenon. It is the assumption that others will see the world as we do. Tom made this mistake: he was blind to the motivations of those in the companies he wanted to merge with. He took the view that they must see the world as he saw it, and, of course, they did not. Atticus Finch, the protagonist lawyer of Harper Lee's novel, '*To Kill a Mockingbird*', said pointedly that 'You never really understand a person until you consider things from his point of view'. The effort to try and see the world as others see it—especially those with whom you might be negotiating, or with whom you might be in conflict—is difficult, but very valuable (see Wang et al. 2014).

Leadership

There is an expensive, modern obsession in organisations with 'leadership' (Alvesson and Spicer 2016), which, when attained, offers a kind of a magic acid to dissolve away the many problems that may arise in business. Leadership is often regarded as a central, vitally important, cloak or a mantle that can be easily adopted when a person is put into a position of leadership. No such obsession exists with 'followership', curiously! In our case study, Tom Spengler is certainly very concerned to show that he is 'a decisive and strong leader'. There are two profound errors that arise as a result of this focus on leadership. The first is one that has already been mentioned, the fundamental attribution error: the mistaking of the person who is at the 'head of the organisation' or system for the system or the organisation itself. The second is the assumption that leadership, when accompanied by some form of charisma, authenticity and capacity to touch individuals at their core, will somehow solve the problems arising within organisations. Many businesses will use language around what it is that a leader is supposed to do. They are supposed to 'make the business world-class' or 'gold standard'; they should be able to entrain or activate the business's 'noble purpose'; they must have a 'vision'; they must be 'thought leaders'; they must be 'horizon scanners'. Time spent on this kind of high-flown activity is, of course, time spent away from engaging in real work.

It is a remarkably underappreciated fact that, in knowledge-based organisations such as professional services firms, universities, research institutes, medical practices or whatever, positions of leadership are rotated. The managing partner, the head of department, or whatever, is seen as a 'first among equals' who is required to behave in a collegiate fashion and bring colleagues along as a whole. Typically their positions are term-limited, and it is no surprise that these kinds of organisations, comprised of very motivated knowledge workers, tend to be among the most stable forms of organisational life that exist today. Universities, for example, have lives that extend back over many centuries. The point here is straightforward: veneration of leadership as *the* solution to what ails a business or an organisation is a strategy that is bound to fail. Leaders have power only to the extent that others grant it to them (Keltner 2016)—leadership is social, at its core. In the modern world, coercive models of leadership will fail—because people can, and do, walk away, leaving the leader bereft of followers. And then where is the leader without followers?

Other Important Cognitive Biases

There are many other cognitive biases; we will explore a few others here. Our memories fail us in all sorts of ways. When judging the frequency of an event, we call the most recent exemplar to mind and use that recall to judge frequency. Thus, the availability in mind of an item is used to judge its frequency. Straight after a plane crash, people when asked how frequent plane crashes are will think of them as being more prevalent than they actually are. Memory is vulnerable to other factors too: learning and recollection are both badly affected by stress and lack of sleep. The language we use is also very important: language has the important property of *'framing'* arguments and discussions. How we speak about something determines in large part how we come to feel about that something. Are immigrants *'welfare tourists'* or are they *'hard-working individuals'* attracted by economic opportunities available in a particular country? The language used 'frames' how we should think of immigration. The crime debate in the UK was dominated in the 1970s by the phrase *'short, sharp, shock'*, which relied on the folk theory that quick and severe punishment would shock teenagers out of criminal tendencies. (The pleasing alliteration of the successive sibilants was an important, but useless, selling point too.) Short, sharp shocks, of course, predictably have no such effect, but why let data from the psychology of punishment and from criminology influence debate? Short, sharp, shock treatments designed to scare adolescents into being good just didn't and don't work. The data we have suggest that adolescents are actually more sensitive to rewards than punishments. The phrase *'cut and run'* was used to forestall debate about the palpably failing US military strategy in Iraq. A change in course couldn't be undertaken until empirical reality forced the change of direction. Verificationism (also known as *confirmation bias* or *myside bias*) is a pervasive and potentially dangerous cognitive error, where evidence favouring a particular point of view is collected and weighted heavily and contrary evidence is discounted or ignored. House prices have been rising for years; therefore, they will continue to rise, so property is a safe-bet investment. Evidence contrary to your point of view is systematically discounted or underweighted, but cherry-picking anecdotes in your favour is not the way to honestly proceed.

Confirmation bias comes with a major problem. It feels good because it activates the brain's reward system (Aue and colleagues 2012). This feeling can easily lead to overconfidence because you are chasing the feeling of intrinsic reward, not systematically pursuing the truth—and the evidence is apparently on your side! The Nobel Prize-winning British scientist, Peter Medawar, warned bluntly against being 'deeply in love' with your ideas and not being willing to expose them to a 'cruelly critical test' in order to discard them as wrong, as quickly as possible (Medawar 1979). Medawar also warned that *the intensity of the conviction that a hypothesis is true has no bearing on whether it is true or not* (ibid, 39). The unwillingness to do so is an interesting cognitive bias—deliberately not exploring counterfactuals or contrary evidence to what you believe or assert, as these other points of view or contrary evidence might *falsify* your claims. Confirmation bias can, with effort, be conquered by its opposite, *falsificationism*, which is a difficult habit of mind to acquire. It is a must for any working scientist. Falsificationism requires considering what empirical evidence would invalidate (falsify) the position you are adopting. One way of avoiding this bias is to state clearly what empirical evidence would falsify your opinion; another is to build an evidence-based brake into policy formation. In science this is done by international, anonymous, expert *'peer review'*. Peer-review and similar systems can be built into the process of deliberation that underlies policy formation or strategic decision-making.

The phrase 'delusional' has sometimes been used to describe the behaviour of certain members of our political parties and businesses, but delusions imply the psychiatric diagnosis of pathological beliefs maintained contrary to all evidence. Anosagnosia (a more useful description taken from neuropsychology) is the condition of literally being *'without knowledge'* (being unaware) of a cognitive or other impairment and behaving as if there is no problem. Additionally, the knowledge and expertise required to solve the problems confronting leadership teams and others may be greater than they can acknowledge, understand and act upon. This leads to anosagnosia within the cultures of these organisations. All sorts of organisations from party political systems to businesses to governments and civil service systems can undervalue expertise and suppress cognitive diversity. In what should have been a publically shameful moment, but wasn't, a former UK Government minister declared during the Brexit debate that *'people in this country have had enough of experts'*. Whatever the merits or demerits of the case for Brexit, the deliberate disparaging of expert knowledge is deeply troublesome. One presumes that the former minister doesn't truly believe what he says, or he would be happy to turn his dental care over to the local chap with a hammer and tongs and take his plane flights with non-qualified pilots (qualified pilots being experts). A list like this where we do have to defer to experts could go on. As we will see in Chapter 7, substantial data show that complex and difficult problems (for example, how to rescue a collapsing economy) are best solved by groups with substantial intellectual strength and capacity (*obvious*), and substantial diversity of experience (*not obvious*).

One final and very important cognitive bias to consider is the *Dunning-Kruger* effect (Dunning and Kruger 1999), named for the psychologists who first described and quantified the effect. This is a bias where the truly incompetent do not realise how truly incompetent they are—they overestimate their own degree of skill and capacity to perform a task requiring expert knowledge. Moreover, their degree of incompetence comes with an important deficiency—they are unable to reflect on their own cognitive processes in such a way as to recognise and appreciate their own mistakes. Technically expressed, they have poor *metacognitive* abilities. This gives rise to the bias of *illusory superiority*: a somewhat ironic bias, because in addition to their poor performance on a task, they will rate their ability as above average. This might be why we all regard ourselves as being better drivers than average! The obverse of this is that those who are highly skilled or expert tend to under-rate and underestimate their own abilities, giving rise to the phenomenon of *illusory inferiority*. The Irish poet, William Butler Yeats, in a famous line from his poem, *The Second Coming*, expresses a version of this pervasive cognitive bias thus: '*The best lack all conviction, while the worst/Are full of passionate intensity.*'

Conclusions

Individual rationality and cognition are limited and error-prone. A system driven by the unrestrained and unhampered cognition of individuals will fail; imposing ideological or personal control where objective, evidence-based and evidence-tested policy formation are called for is a recipe for disaster. *And we know this, but this is the mistake we repeatedly make.* Thus, our institutions and organisations must be re-engineered to be adaptive, plastic and capable of learning (and especially to be capable of learning and acting upon upsetting and unpleasant truths). Robust institutional governance processes are required to recognise error and failure quickly and to change course rapidly. Organisational design needs to recognise our biases; these biases need to be tested robustly and our ideologies discarded when they fail empirical tests.

Exercises

1. List some common examples of cognitive biases that are apparent during the debate around a salient political or business problem. Politicians provide a target rich focus—so pick an important debate (such as Brexit) and list some of the more common biases exhibited by politicians.
2. How would you address the persistence of these biases? Are there changes to deliberative processes that could be introduced that would make a difference?
3. If you have taken one side in the debate (say that you are pro-Brexit, for example), challenge your thinking, first, by laying out in 500 words or so your pro-Brexit case. Now, and this is hard, set out a 500-word case for the anti-Brexit case. Then, set out the empirical information that would cause you to change your mind.
4. Given a course of action that is failing in your business, set out a course of action that allows you to change course.
5. Are there other biases that Tom Spengler was prone to? What do the CEOs of the companies that he hoped to merge with need to watch out for in their own cognition—do they have obvious cognitive biases also?

Further Reading

Alvesson M, Spicer A (2016) The stupidity paradox: The power and pitfalls of functional stupidity at work. Profile Books, London, UK.

Aue T, Nusbaum HC, Cacioppo JT (2012) Neural correlates of wishful thinking. *Soc Cogn Affect Neurosci.*, 7:991–1000. doi: 10.1093/scan/nsr081

Benson, B (2017). Cognitive bias cheat sheet, simplified. https://medium.com/thinking-is-hard/4-conundrums-of-intelligence-2ab78d90740f.

Dunning D, Johnson K, Ehrlinger J, Kruger J (2003) Why people fail to recognize their own incompetence. Curr. Dir. Psychol. Sci., 12:83–87. doi: 10.1111/1467-8721.01235.

Henrich J, Mcelreath R, Barr A, Ensminger J, Barrett C, Bolyanatz A, Cardenas JC, Gurven M, Gwako E, Henrich N, Lesorogol C, Marlowe F, Tracer D, Ziker J (2006) Costly punishment across human societies. *Science*, 312:1767–1770. People from 15 different cultures are all willing to punish others who exhibit selfish behavior that increases societal inequity, but the extent varies widely. doi: 10.1126/science.1127333.

Kahan DM (2007) Culture and identity-protective cognition: Explaining the white male effect in risk perception. Faculty Scholarship Series. Paper 101. http://digitalcommons.law.yale.edu/fss_papers/101

Kahneman D (2011) Thinking, fast and slow. Farrar, Straus and Giroux, New York.

Keltner D (2016) The power paradox: How we gain and lose influence. Penguin/Allen Lane, London.

Kruger J, Dunning D (1999) Unskilled and unaware of it: How difficulties in recognizing one's own incompetence lead to inflated self-assessments. J Pers Soc Psychol, 77(6):1121–1134. CiteSeerX 10.1.1.64.2655Freely accessible. doi: 10.1037/0022-3514.77.6.1121.

Medawar PB (1979) Advice to a young scientist. Basic Books, New York.

Nisbett RE (2015) Mindware: Tools for smart thinking. Farrar, Straus and Giroux, New York.

Tom SM, Fox CR, Trepel C, Poldrack RA (2007) The neural basis of loss aversion in decision-making under risk. *Science*, 315:515–518. Overlapping brain networks respond more to gambling losses than to gains, correlating with behavioral observations about risk aversion. doi: 10.1126/science.1134239.

Wang CS, Tai K, Ku G, Galinsky AD (2014) Perspective-taking increases willingness to engage in intergroup contact. *PLoS ONE*, 9(e85681). doi: 10.1371/journal.pone.0085681.

6

Person Perception—How Others See Us, How We See Leaders

This chapter explores how group deliberation and group decision-making occur and how we more or less automatically define status within groups. It also explores how, paradoxically, the mechanisms used for person perception and status determination are also the same mechanisms that are used for brand perception.

Being Human: The Frontal Lobes and Intentional Behaviour

Social organisation and social life are central to human life and human affairs. The very structure of our brains has determined the complexity of our social world. Our outsized frontal lobes have driven the organisation of our capacity for intentional behaviour in our social world—how we understand the intentions of others and how we regulate our behaviour regarding others. The story of the brain-injured patient, Phineas Gage, is one of the most famous case studies within modern brain science; his story is one that every student of the frontal lobes is expected to know. Gage's case illustrates much about how functions that we think are intrinsic to us as human beings can be localised to a particular region of the brain and how these functions can be lost or changed because of damage to those regions. Gage's story came to light as a result of an accident during railway construction in the state of Vermont. He had a dramatic and appalling accident when a tamping iron (used for packing dynamite powder into holes for rock-blasting), about

2.5 cm wide and 1.1 m long, entered at high-velocity through his left cheekbone and ripped through his left frontal lobe, probably removing it almost entirely and almost certainly causing extensive damage to his right frontal lobe. Astonishingly, Gage survived this extreme example of a penetrating head injury and lived for another 11 or so years. Gage's physician Dr John Harlow wrote a short description of the change in Gage's personality resulting from the damage to his frontal lobes. He wrote that Gage became *'fitful, irreverent, indulging at times in the grossest profanity (that was not previously his custom), manifesting but little deference for his fellows, impatient of restraint or advice when it conflicts with his desires, at times pertinaciously obstinate, yet capricious and vacillating, devising many plans of future operations, which are no sooner arranged than they are abandoned in turn for others appearing more feasible. A child in his intellectual capacity and manifestations, he has the animal passions of a strong man. Previous to his injury, although untrained in the schools, he possessed a well-balanced mind, and was looked upon by those who knew him as a shrewd, smart businessman, very energetic and persistent in executing all his plans of operation. In this regard his mind was radically changed, so decidedly that his friends and acquaintances said he was 'no longer Gage.'*

Gage's case shows us many things. Trivially, it shows that despite severe brain damage, if the location of the damage avoids certain key brain areas needed to sustain vital functions, a human brain and body can live through and with appalling damage. Much less trivially, Gage's case was a breakthrough case in defining the relationship between certain brain functions—the executive functions—that are localisable to particular brain regions and networks. Gage's case allows us to go much further and ask questions about the essential nature of our personalities and humanity, which we can now start to answer with reference to the brain. The usefulness of Gage's case lies primarily in its ability to show us how the attributes that define us as uniquely human and different from other species can be broken down into their components. In turn, these components provide us with rules of thumb (heuristics) that can be used to interpret (and perhaps predict) human behaviour.

What would a (partial) list of the attributes of being human that render us different from other species consist of? Any reasonable list would probably include at least the following: the capacity to formulate intentions; to plan actions; to make moral judgements; to imagine alternative pasts and futures (counterfactual thinking); to know of our own eventual personal death; to forego immediate rewards in favour of future ones; to be able to infer the mental states of others. Where do these capacities reside? The answer in modern brain science is increasingly given as in the frontal lobes, often acting in concert with other brain regions. The frontal lobes are, as their name implies, the lobes of the brain situated at the front of the head, behind the forehead and between the temples. The frontal lobes are massively over-developed in humans compared to our closest non-human primate relatives (bonobos, chimpanzees, and so on). In turn these non-human primate species generally and comfortably out-rank other animal species in terms of frontal lobe size. The frontal lobes are sometimes referred to as having 'executive functions' within the context of the operation of the whole brain. Executive functions consist of those capacities that enable a person to engage successfully in independent, purposive self-serving behaviour. Purposive, self-serving behaviour includes the capacity to formulate goals; to plan and organise goal-directed behaviour; to carry out such behaviour fully and effectively and to monitor and self-correct behaviour. A natural question is why these lobes are so big in humans and in our close non-human primate relatives. One answer is that the size of our frontal lobes directly relates to the complexity of the social world within which we live.

Spontaneous Emergence of Groups and Organisations

Humans naturally and spontaneously organise into groups, organisations and other institutions (Fiske 2011). We all more-or-less automatically rank our own status and the status of others within these groups. This should not a surprise—we seek promotions and career advancement; we long to see the teams we support rise up the rankings; we give prizes and other markers of status to exemplary performers. Position on rankings often determines rewards for the individual and the group. These rankings have profound effects on performance within the group—for better and for worse. Brain and behaviour has an important impact on the organisational context because we focus automatically on status (what is it; how we do it; how it inscribed on our brains) and social comparison (why we make comparisons; how compar-ison and status markers informs, protects and help us fit into organisations). We need to self-consciously examine the costs and benefits of such status comparisons in organisational life, and translate these lessons into how organisational life is designed.

Humans are a profoundly social species—this is such a truism that it almost has the status of a cliché. Nonetheless, it is true, and we organise work, family, social, sporting and other aspects of our lives around groups of differing sizes and scales. These groups tend to prefer face-to-face interaction and have close cohesion. We have evolved over the ages to work together and to get along together. We have brain mechanisms that support our functioning in a social world, that allow us to attribute mental states and agency to other human beings, and that allow us to define in-group and out-group members rapidly and efficiently. We also define our status within groups quickly and efficiently, and we use group organisational forms that allow leadership to rapidly emerge. Leadership is a complex topic on which there is a vast empirical literature. Here, I will focus the discussion of leadership around a narrow range of topics: how leaders are perceived and the brain mechanisms that underlie this perception.

Brain and Behavioural Sciences Approaches to Understanding Leadership

Leadership is an all-pervasive phenomenon in both human and animal societies. Leadership emerges because it solves important and difficult problems for groups and organisations. The groups can be diverse: they can be birds flying in a particular direction; predators organising themselves to attack their prey; they can be schoolchildren on the playground; families, social friendship circles; and of course organisations such as government, businesses, churches, political parties and the military. Leadership emerges quickly in groups, even in groups that are palpably failing or are in trouble, such as political parties that are losing electoral support. In the United Kingdom, for example, the Conservative Party lost power in 1997, accompanied by a devastating loss in seats, and had great difficulty in redefining their mission as a political party in the twenty-first century. In their 13 years out of power, they lost three general elections decisively and, as a consequence, disposed of three leaders. Finally, after being out of power for three election cycles, the Conservatives were elected back into government again, in coalition with the Liberal Democrats, in 2010 and as a single party government in 2015. The Liberal Democrats, in turn, went on to be devastated in the election of 2015, but yet were still able to find within themselves a leader to carry on the flag of the much-diminished party. And in the post-Brexit period the Conservatives disposed of and replaced their leader, quickly and efficiently. Similar tales are to be told about political parties, businesses and other institutions worldwide. The key point here is that although the institution itself is failing (or, at least, not succeeding), there is no shortage of people willing to assume the position of leader. The *iron law of institutions* is the name given to the concern of people who have power in institutions to preserve their power within that institution (*even when the institution itself is palpably failing*) rather than being concerned with the success of the institution itself. This is often why removing people from a position of leadership for which they are demonstrably unsuitable is so fraught with difficulty: the rules of the game are usually set up to favour those who hold the position of power. And even when the leader is removed, there is no guarantee that the change of leadership will make things better. Leadership, as previously mentioned, is not a magic acid that somehow dissolves away organisational problems.

Leadership is seen as desirable in itself, and there is always a perpetual jockeying for position and preferment in order to succeed to leadership. Of course, those who wish to be leaders give less thought than they should to what happens when eventually they stop being leaders—that happens too! And there is an important need to think about leadership models—these can and should vary dramatically, depending on the needs of the organisation. The 'leader takes all' model of autocracies is clearly unworkable in the democracies of today, despite the occasional resurgence of populism. Leadership in 'knowledge worker' organisations takes on a much different form. In universities, research institutes and professional firms (such as law, accounting, consulting and medicine), leadership positions are most often held for short periods of time (say three to six years). Managing partners, heads of department, deans and others are seen as transiently 'first among equals', and their job is not to 'lead' the very self-motivated and mobile individuals that work in these positions. Leadership is often rotated and often seen as something to be avoided, because it gets in the way of doing one's own, more interesting, work.

What Do Leaders Do?

There are two separate questions to be addressed here: the first is what problems leadership solves; the second is when leadership positions are attained, what are the consequences of being a leader for both the leader themselves and their followers? Leadership solves problems—or, at least, that is what leadership is supposed to do. By providing a singular focus for an organisation, leaders are able to provide decisions about resource allocation (who gets the goodies: who doesn't); the direction of movement of the group (this can be the physical direction of the group, as in a sergeant leading a platoon into battle or a team captain providing a direction of movement for their team players); or it can be intellectual (that is, framing an overall mission and goal for the organisation, allowing it to speak to itself in ways that develop and sustain its unique culture and that then allows it to present itself as a brand to the outside world). Another very vital role played by leaders is in conflict mediation. Leaders are often given privileges of making decisions that are decisive and that do not allow dissent. This decision-making capacity afforded a leader can arise from at least two sources. The first is the formal authority they occupy as a result of the position they hold, and this allows them to exercise decision-making in ways that others lower down the hierarchy are incapable of engaging in. The second arises from their personal characteristics, the extent to which they are respected, regarded warmly and regarded as competent in terms of how they present themselves. These roles are not just inward-facing where the organisation is concerned. They are also outward-facing, for a key role of leaders is also to mediate between groups and to create opportunities for their own organisation to prosper and thrive. Leaders, in summary, are tasked with resolving the problems experienced by groups, and they are tasked with providing a singular focus for the organisation—and the key phrase here is 'organisation'. Individuals within the company, the business, the institution, occupy roles that are subordinate to that of the leader and that may lead them to be directly or indirectly answerable to the expectations and goals set by the leader. Thus, leaders provide a singular focus for the organisation as the 'chief officers' of that organisation.

Formal positions of leadership can be attained in a variety of ways, from succession planning, through incumbency as the result of the de novo creation of a new organisation, to elections, to boardroom coups, through coercion or other means. The outcome of this process, however, returns to a set of predictable processes. Other persons within the organisation, and indeed outside the organisation, will judge the new leader, and they will judge the new leader rapidly and in predictable ways. Newly emergent leaders, therefore, need to actively manage how they present themselves internally and externally. The key question, therefore, for a new leader is how they manage this self-presentation (to the extent that they can) and then how others will perceive this self-presentation. No one can control this complex process because unpredictable factors will intrude. There are some ways in which leaders or 'leaders to be' can influence this complex process, though. To succeed as a leader, one major review (Haslem and colleagues

2011) suggests successful leadership requires obeying a few simple precepts. Leaders must be sensitive to their followers, support them, treat them with respect and exceed their expectations; be positive and inspirational; work hard and be seen to work hard for the group; and not be overbearing or arrogant. Which of our leaders, past and present, can tick off these precepts successfully? The power associated with leadership tends to act against these attributes. This may of course be why knowledge worker organisations are very good at constraining the power of leaders within their organisations.

Judging Others: We Are *'Cognitive Misers'*

Consider the following situations. You are walking down the street at night. It's a little bit dark, and a figure emerges from the shadows in front of you. You have to make a very quick decision: does this person seem to be somebody that I need to worry about, or is it somebody that I can ignore? Better yet, is the shape shambling towards you a friend that you agreed to meet earlier on? Immediately you make that decision; your feelings change. You may feel warm towards the person who is coming towards you; you may feel fear towards the person who is coming towards you. Consider a different situation: you are somehow the newly installed leader (i.e. CEO) of the freshly created Germane-Levenson Biopharma (Tom Spengler is indisposed, after all). The shareholders have been restive and have elected, at the last AGM, some new executive directors, as they are entitled to do under your company's share subscription rules. Your company is in trouble, as it has been losing money quarter-on-quarter. The merged entity just isn't working very well. You have been given the job of turning it around, and you meet these new directors for the first time at your board meeting. You shake hands, and what do you think? You make a quick judgement about whether or not these people are your enemy or are your friend. You make a quick judgement as to whether or not they see you as the problem, or you as the solution. These processes are remarkably quick and they typically happen in about a second to a second and a half (Fiske 2011). The implication is that our brain picks out a very few salient features and classifies these individuals quickly and consistently. Indeed, there is little more frustrating a position to be in, when a possible situation of conflict presents itself, that the person before you is someone that you can't 'read'. What you're actually saying is that this person is someone whom you can't classify and whose behaviour you believe you are going to find difficult to predict.

Making Person Judgements: They're Quick and Relatively Automatic

How do we make these judgements? To put it another way, how does our brain make these judgements? In what must be one of the most remarkable discoveries in neuroscience in the past few decades, we now know that the brain has a 'mentalising network', which allows us to make rapid judgements about others, and to do so on the basis of remarkably little effort and remarkably little information (Fiske 2011). In other words, we are 'cognitive misers', and we dislike expending much energy in making these judgements (a good example of Kahneman's 'System 1' at work). We make snap decisions regarding other people along two dimensions. The first is how the other person makes us feel. Do they make us feel warmly towards them? Do they make us feel coldly towards them, or some intermediate position along this warm-cold dimension? This judgement is typically made in just under a second. We then make another judgement with regard to the person's agency, that is to say, their ability to carry out their intentions. Are they capable and competent or incapable and incompetent—i.e. can they carry out their intentions toward you? This judgement takes about 1.2 seconds to emerge.

The speed and rapidity of these judgements suggest that the brain processes involved are very swift indeed, from perceiving movement, to seeing a face, to judging the position of the hands and feet, to judging the gait and movement of the other individual, to judging their clothing. All of these things must be processed quickly and reliably. After all, if you make this judgement too slowly, and you mistake that yellow blob for a bush when it's actually a tiger, you won't have left many descendants around. So these mechanisms are honed by evolution and they are conserved in the brains of humans. Clever brain imaging experiments by, among others, Susan Fiske and her colleagues suggest that we have a brain area that makes judgements about competence and a brain area that makes judgements about warmth. Fiske refers to this capacity as a 'stereotype content model' (or SCM). Intuitively, we have some sense that these dimensions exist. We all know individuals that we walk away from feeling good about ourselves, but whom we wouldn't necessarily put in charge of running our business. Similarly, we know individuals whom we don't particularly like, they don't make us feel good, but we would be very happy to have them running our business. Then, we occasionally come across paragons of humanity who both make us feel good and whom we would trust to run our business. And then, occasionally, we come across individuals who neither make us feel good nor whom we trust. These are the two dimensions that we typically classify the people we meet into.

Status Within Organisations

In addition to rapidly classifying individuals along the cold/warmth and competent/incompetent dimensions, humans do something else that is quite remarkable. We also rapidly assign people relative positions within groups. Think about the first time you walked into a group of people that you didn't know. Quickly, people rank each other as leaders, as followers, as wise voices, as slightly off-beam, along all sorts of dimensions, and we do this rapidly and quickly. Susan Fiske (2011) captures this dynamic beautifully in the title of her book '*Envy Up, Scorn Down*'. This title captures something very important about how humans interact with each other. In addition to more-or-less automatically classifying each other, we also have a need for status, and we need to figure out where we are in terms of our status within the groups that we define ourselves as being part of. The groups themselves can be very arbitrarily constructed. These can be fans of football teams, members of political parties, or whatever, but the dynamic itself is reliable and replicable, and it is that people will use markers of warmth and competence in order to define each other's status within a group. One such marker, which we will meet again, for status is IQ, or a proxy for IQ, namely education, or even something simpler, such as the speed and quality of one's verbal articulacy.

The Brain Processes Underlying the Stereotype Content Model

Brain imaging has proven to be a great boon to modern behavioural and brain sciences because when experimental designs are clever, brain imaging can allow us to uncover processes that may not have been previously suspected. We have seen this before in the discovery of the default mode network—the brain network that is most active in our brain, most of the time. How do we study processes like social comparison and social judgement using brain imaging? In principle, the procedure is relatively straightforward. You are brought to a laboratory and placed within a modern brain imaging system, and you are asked to make a series of simple, straightforward and rapid judgements of images presented to you of differing individuals' faces. These images would be very diverse, they may include well-known public figures, they may include individuals about whom you have no knowledge whatsoever, they might be individuals who are exemplars of particular social groups, such as athletes, or they might be individuals from the army, they might be individuals who apparently are bankers, they might be drug addicts, alcoholics, teachers or whoever. On a response pad, you simply make a snap judgement: do these people evoke feelings of cold or warmth within you? And are they individuals who also evoke feelings of competence or incompetence within you? We might, for example, classify our national Olympic athletes as individuals who evoke feelings of warmth and pride, and also feelings of competence, whereas a football team that we may particularly despise might evoke feelings of competence (because they are good) but also feelings of coldness because we dislike them and we have no loyalty to them. Remarkably, what we see is that for judgements of three groups we get a common pattern of activation in the brain. For individuals that we judge as incompetent but warm (think Homer Simpson), individuals who evoke warmth and competence (think Marge Simpson or Lisa Simpson), or individuals who evoke coldness but competence (think Mr Burns, the nuclear power plant owner in the Simpsons), the same brain areas in the brain's mentalising network are activated. This is a set of areas along the midline of the brain. There is one remarkable and consistent difference, though. For people who evoke judgements of coldness (we do not feel well-disposed towards them) and incompetence (we don't think they are very good at carrying out their intentions) (think, Comic Book Guy, or Mad Cat Lady in *The Simpsons*) we see an activation in a completely different brain area, one that is on both sides of the brain (the insula), a brain area typically activated during feelings of disgust or illness or sickness. In Fiske's studies, individuals who appear to be homeless, to be dirty or to be addicts, or indeed all three of these altogether, typically show activations in the insula and also are ranked as evoking feelings of coldness and incompetence.

The key thing here, however, is not that these feelings are intrinsically evoked by the individual, but they are evoked by the feeling that the ranked individual is a member of some out-group. The out-group is learned through the culture one grows up in: think the enmity expressed by the supporters of one football team for the supporters of another football team—even if they both come from the same geographic locale (Manchester City versus Manchester United supporters, or Rangers versus Celtic supporters, for example). When we see this out-group categorisation we typically do not judge members of this group as being fully human. We do not attribute to them agency, and we do not attribute to them a full mental life of the type that we ascribe to members of our own in-group (however that may be defined).

As an exercise, over the next few minutes try and generate some examples of cold and competent out-groups. These might include, for example, moneylenders (who are very efficient at extracting cash that they have lent to others, usually under a real threat of duress), or perhaps bankers, or some such group. Others might include insurance salespeople, who are very good at selling products to you that you may not necessarily want. Write down a few others. If you are in the UK, where would you rank the current leaders of the major political parties? Similarly, if you are in the US, where would you rank the current leaders of the Democratic and Republican parties? Note that your judgement will be moderated dramatically by your prior political affiliation. If it is the case that you are a Conservative Party voter, we can predict what your likely feelings are towards the current Labour Party leader. Similarly, if you are a Republican voter, your feelings towards the current Democratic Party leaders are likely to be very predictable. There are exceptions of course. During the heyday of Tony Blair's premiership in the late 1990s, and before he became entangled in the Iraq war, he evoked feelings of warmth and competence even in the opposition, who were desperately frustrated with their own leadership and its incapacity to deliver a win at successive general elections. There is a further lesson here, which is this: if your own organisation regards you, as the leader, as being both cold and incompetent, you will not be long in the position of leader.

What Does the Brain Think of Brands?

Take a random sample of some of the product and service brands that might go through your mind (for example, Coca Cola, Johnson and Johnson, BP, Volkswagen, Google, Apple, Marlboro, Guinness, or PWC). What happens when you think about '*brands*' as opposed to '*persons*'? It turns out that when we ask people to make judgements about brands, the same brain networks are activated as are activated when we ask people to make judgements about other people. In other words, *brands are also people* (at least as far as the mentalising network of the brain is concerned). This means we conceive of brands as having similar properties to people. Brands can make us feel good and brands can make us feel bad. We regard brands as embodying competence or incompetence. And more than this, brands, just like people, can undergo sudden and rapid changes in their brand position in terms of the stereotype model very quickly and rapidly.

A recent fine example illustrating the damage that can be done to a brand was the unravelling of BP's reputation as it struggled to handle the Deepwater Horizon oilrig explosion and the resulting Gulf of Mexico oil spill in April 2010. It came across as neither competent nor caring. Its then Chief Executive Officer, Tony Hayward was heard to say '*I'm sorry. We're sorry for the massive disruption it's caused their lives. There's no one who wants this over more than I do. I'd like my life back.*' These words were seen as callous and uncaring, especially coming after the deaths of 11 men who wouldn't be getting their lives back, and the apology was widely seen as forced and insincere. Hayward was eventually forced from his position, but the fallout for BP continued to be substantial. In stark contrast, Johnson and Johnson continues to be one of the world's most trusted brands, despite what could have been a customer relations disaster when one of its prominent over-the-counter medicines, Tylenol, was found to have been tampered with, and people were poisoned as a result. Johnson and Johnson, under the leadership team of then CEO, James E. Burke, quickly and competently moved to get ahead of the problems that it faced, and did so in rapid time, showing that it both cared about its customers (evoking feelings of warmth) and was capable of dealing with the problem quickly and summarily (thereby generating feelings of competence).

Companies Are People Too

As we've seen, the mentalising network of the brain ascribes agency and warmth to individuals (or not, as the case may be). Brands evoke similar kinds of feelings, but it also turns out that companies evoke similar feelings, when we are asked to judge the actions of companies. This is different from the feelings that a brand may evoke—it is how we feel about the *behaviour* of the company. The neuroscientist David Eagleman and his colleagues at Baylor College of Medicine have conducted a very clever experiment contrasting judgements about persons, companies or things. In a nice variation of the experiments conducted by Susan Fiske and her colleagues, Eagleman and his colleagues (see Pick et al. 2014) had volunteers come to the laboratory and imaged their brains while they were making judgements about the actions of persons or things, or about companies. Examples of the vignettes used by Eagleman and his colleagues in their experiments included the following:

1. Jane is an elderly woman living on her own and has been bed ridden for the last several months. John was hired to take care of her lawn. Knowing that Jane would not be able to check on the condition of her lawn, John continues charging her for service though he no longer shows up. (Negative person condition)
2. Jane is an elderly woman living on her own and has been bed ridden for the last several months. Baxefu is her lawn care company. Knowing that Jane would not be able to check on the condition of her lawn, Baxefu continues charging her for service though they no longer show up. (Negative company condition)
3. A crossword is a word puzzle that normally takes the form of a rectangular grid of white and shaded squares. The goal is to fill the white squares with letters, forming words or phrases, by solving clues, which lead to the answers. Shaded squares are used to separate the words or phrases. (Neutral condition)

They examined the intensity of the emotions experienced by people about companies and people who behaved well or behaved badly. Eagleman and colleagues report that their volunteers had approximately similar emotions regarding the actions of persons and companies. Crucially, they did not experience these emotions about things (crosswords and the like). They also found that the mentalising network was activated when their volunteers made judgements about the actions of persons and companies, but not about things.

These findings shouldn't be entirely surprising, because there is a long tradition in western law of regarding companies as 'legal persons'. In fact, Trinity College, Dublin, where I work, was founded in 1592 as a *body corporate*. This also provides a clue as to the longevity of institutions such as universities, armies or, indeed, companies. Successful institutions have a life and a brand independent of the individuals who make up their component parts. Such institutions or organisations have a legal identity that animates them independently of the individuals comprising the institution. This provides the answer, of course, to the old conundrum: if by a miracle, or some happenstance event, all the students and staff disappeared from a university, would that mean the university itself has disappeared? The answer is no; it has a legal and corporate existence that would continue to be recognised by individuals outside the university, and when it would be repopulated again, it would be repopulated by individuals using the organisational plan, the processes, the procedures, and the rules that comprised that university. Institutions all over the world are studded with entities that have a continuing legal or corporate existence, even though the entity itself has to all intents and purposes ceased to exist. There are innumerable trusts in existence with no known beneficiaries; innumerable bank accounts with no known beneficiaries; there are titles to land bound up with complicated trusts, established hundreds of years ago for a particular purpose, which continue to exist and have a legal organisational and corporate life, despite the fact that there are no humans there to animate them. This even occurs for investment vehicles. Perpetual bonds and 100-year bonds are sold to institutions in the full knowledge that the individuals who are buying them will have long since departed the earth when these bonds are either due to mature or continue to pay out in perpetuity. Finally, it is the case that, according to Eagleman's data at least, we do (happily) feel more strongly in our emotional judgements about people than we do about companies. Eagleman shows this in two ways: the intensity of the activation scene in the brain when making judgements about companies is less than those seen when making judgements about individuals and the intensity of the rating given. It would be a little bit strange if this were otherwise, but it is good to see this appear in the data.

Putting It All Together

So, let's tie together the implications of the foregoing discussion. First, humans are cognitive misers (that is, we like to conserve energy) because we use the same brain circuits for judging people, brands and organisations. These brain circuits allow us to judge people based on how we perceive their warmth and competence, and we make judgements about brands on exactly the same dimensions. We experience similar emotions regarding the actions of persons and companies, but we feel more strongly in our judgements about people compared to companies.

Where does this leave leaders? Leaders have a particular set of problems. Leaders are judged in a twofold fashion as persons and as brands. This is necessarily the case. The CEO of a multinational company employing 80,000 or 100,000 people will never be in a position to meet all of the employees of that company, even if the CEO conducts town hall meetings *ad nauseam* in every geographical territory that the company works in. But the CEO will meet direct reports and will have indirect interactions with a wide variety of people. Therefore, the CEO has to project a particular image within the company and beyond the company to its peer companies, competitors, regulators and others, but also has to manage how they interact with the people they rub shoulders with on an hourly, daily and weekly basis. CEOs spend most of their days in meetings and rarely get more than 15 minutes at a time uninterrupted. This means that CEOs must be people-oriented and they must be capable of managing their interactions with others in ways that those others find fulfilling, or they will find themselves without others to interact with in short order. Thus, CEOs, leaders and others face a double judgement. They are judged individually as persons, and they are also judged as a brand, what it is that they represent. A good leader, therefore, must be able to engage in social metacognition. That is, they should be able to read the likely responses of the larger public, stakeholders and others beyond the boardroom and then, having read those, anticipate how they should respond in order to respond appropriately. Given the demands placed upon leaders, it is not surprising that so many of them fail at their task. Equally, it is not surprising that so many of them spend time focusing on their core strengths—usually the areas that they have trained in, whether this be finance, coding or whatever—but neglecting the essential people skills that they actually require to prosper in the modern world. It is little surprise, therefore, that so many CEOs and other leaders commit so many gaffes in respect to their interactions with others. This is not merely the effect of erratic impulse control resulting from fatigue, exasperation or exhaustion: it may also reflect the long period of training with a particular skill set that has allowed the CEO or other leader to prosper, but which is now largely redundant in the new context they find themselves in.

Exercises

1. Think about the last time you sat beside someone you didn't know. How did you feel? What did you think about them? How quickly did these feelings and thoughts occur for you?
2. Watch a television programme you don't normally watch, with the sound off. Note what you think and feel about two or three of the principal characters on the screen. Now, turn the sound on, so you can hear their voices. How do you perceive them now?
3. Think of a fictional character you especially like or hate on a television programme. Write down words and phrases you associate with them. You

do know they are fictional—but yet they evoke strong feelings nonetheless. Repeat this exercise for a character from a novel.

4. Write out the names of a few political leaders—push yourself on this. Go beyond the leadership of the few countries you know well. Look up the names of leaders of countries you may know well, but whose leaders you do not (pick a few countries in hemispheres you haven't visited recently). Critically, do this *using image search only.* How do you feel about these leaders? Now—write down what you *know* about these leaders. Now—check out whether what you think you know is true. Do you understand your person judgement mechanisms a little better now?

5. You are the press officer for a major company that has launched self-driving cars. You have to manage the public relations disaster because of a major flaw in the software of your cars, which causes them to drive through junctions where pedestrians have priority. Inevitably, some pedestrians have been injured and killed. Write the bullet points for the briefing documents that your company CEO has to deliver.

6. You are the Chair of the Board of Directors of the self-driving car company in point number 4. Your CEO keeps going off message and doesn't understand what the problem is. What do you do to prevent a public relations disaster and save your company from bankruptcy?

7. Write down the words and phrases that occur to you regarding how Tom Spengler thinks of his own public self-presentation as a leader.

8. How status-driven is Tom Spengler?

Further Reading

Fiske ST (2011) Envy up, scorn down: How status divides us. Russell Sage Foundation, New York.

Haslam SA, Reicher SD, Platow, MJ (2011) The new psychology of leadership identity, influence and power. Psychology Press, Guildford, UK.

Plitt, M, Savjani, RR, Eagleman, DM (2014) Are corporations people too? The neural correlates of moral judgments about companies and individuals. Soc. Neurosci., 10:113–125. http://dx.doi.org/10.1080/17470919.2014.978026

7

Working in Groups and Teams: Group Deliberations

Humans are a social species, and humans organise spontaneously into groups. Group behaviour is something we share with other non-human primate species. Certain principles are starting to emerge from studies of group structure, formation and behaviour. Group meetings of every type and stripe are a ubiquitous feature of organisational life. Peter Drucker, the renowned management theorist, famously stated *'Meetings are a symptom of bad organization. The fewer meetings the better'*. He had it right *and* wrong. Coming together in meetings and in other, less formal, places (such as 'the water cooler', coffee bar or wherever) is an essential part of maintaining the *social disposition* of organisations. I use the phrase 'social disposition' deliberately. Organisations, at their core, are social: they rely on the patterns of interactions among the individuals that work in those organisations to ensure that the organisation achieves its goal, whatever this goal may be. Humans are a profoundly social species. This is a theme reiterated time and again throughout this book. Social learning and social transmission of knowledge, on a one-to-one or small group basis, form an essential and core part of how it is that we learn during the course of both childhood and adolescence, but also how we learn in organisations. So all is well then, isn't it? Unfortunately not. Survey after survey of employees indicates that meetings can be among the least productive and most complained-about activities that employees complain about. Complaints take myriad forms, from meetings with no apparent agenda, to meetings that have no apparent conclusion, to meetings whose minutes do not meaningfully reflect the discussion that has just taken part, to meetings where the boss spends their time bullying and harassing

© The Author(s) 2018
S. O'Mara, *A Brain for Business – A Brain for Life*, The Neuroscience of Business, https://doi.org/10.1007/978-3-319-49154-7_7

individual employees, in the mistaken belief that this will in some way encourage better performance in others. Steve Jobs is the archetypal example of this kind of boss, so much so that his employees referred to his '*reality distortion field*', which surrounded many of the things that he would do and say. And of course, when we look back on his amazing career, we tend now to just focus on his successes and forget his many failures.

There are at least two ways to think of how it is that meetings fail. One is in terms of the economic cost and opportunity cost of the meeting. Let's look at the economic cost and opportunity cost first. Think of a professional services firm such as a law firm or a management consultancy. It may have a number of so-called fee-earners (the professionals whose time can be directly charged on a project basis or an hourly basis to some piece of client-originating work). In addition, these individuals may have support staff, personal assistants, junior lawyers or the like; then, they have an attributable part of the cost of running the business as well (things like the electricity bills, the cost of their building, professional indemnity and other similar kinds of costs). Let's say, for the sake of example, these individuals are paid on average gross salary of €200 per hour. That means a meeting of one hour's duration with ten such individuals involved costs €2,000 of their time. Furthermore, their time might be charged out at, say, €350 per hour. Time spent in a routine office meeting can't be charged to a client, so the gross cost is in fact €2,000 plus €3,500—in other words, €5,500. It gets worse. Taking people away from their work also breaks the pattern of their working day, so there is an *opportunity cost* also deriving from taking them away from the work that they are engaged in. This might be difficult to capture directly, but it could manifest itself in things such as ideas that were not had for the court case that was about to be fought, and therefore lost (a hidden though palpable opportunity cost), or, in the case of a knowledge worker such as a computer coder, the time away from what might have been a breakthrough moment that would have led to a faster, better, cheaper, more efficient method of delivering some service. These are many costs for a business to bear. My example, if anything, understates the matter. Michael Mankins and his colleagues (2014), for example, found that, in one large organisation they examined, the total cost in terms of time of the weekly executive meeting was an astonishing 300,000 hours per annum. This happens because of a ripple or cascade effect through the organisation of staff needing to service, in an upward fashion, the informational and other demands of the top-tier of management. Therefore, meetings, when they are held, should be held sparingly; they should be useful, productive and carefully structured so that the meeting achieves some meaningful goal or aim. Businesses and organisations should attempt to ensure when it decides to hold meetings that these meetings are capable of meeting these types of exacting criteria.

Meetings Going Awry

The example I examine here is a straightforward one. Consider mid-level, interregional management meetings in a large pharmaceutical company, employing several tens of thousands of workers. Managers who are requested to attend those meetings, in addition to losing time in the office, will also spend time in the air, time in the hotel and time engaged in preparation for the meeting, which may be entirely wasted or pointless. Additionally, there is transit time to and from the meeting, settling-in time in the meeting and perhaps other time costs arising from the meeting also. Flights can be delayed or cancelled; taxis may not be available; trains may breakdown, or whatever. There are also the lost hours of productivity resulting from a lack of clearly defined goals as a result of the meeting or from bullying or harassment that can occur during the meeting. Again, to emphasise the point, meetings should be held sparingly, they should be useful, and they should be productive. They should leave participants feeling that they have gained more from attending the meeting than they lost from being at the meeting, and they should leave individuals with at least some sense of a common or shared purpose in the greater organisation itself.

We have all been there: having a difficult and ill-focused discussion where it is not clear what the source of division is and from where it is difficult to achieve a shared outcome. The important lesson from this section is simple: when a meeting is drifting toward conflict, and it is obvious that there is a problem with communication, not necessarily with the topics at hand, stop the conversation or discussion. State clearly, but politely that what is being said is not necessarily what is being heard. Ask the other party to state what it is that they think you are saying. Try to achieve a shared statement that reflects the underlying content and intent of all parties present. The effect of these strategies will be in effect to re-boot the brains of all present: the language areas of the brain will be re-engaged, but with a new task.

Why do meetings fail? Meetings fail because there are ubiquitous tendencies in both our thinking and our behaviour, arising from cognitive biases on the one hand, and status biases on the other, that can serve to derail a meeting quite badly. Chairing and running a meeting is a skill, one that requires some degree of learning and the ability to take the perspective of others. If you think the meeting was a great success because you chaired it and spoke a lot, then you're wrong. During the meeting, did you notice that after a few minutes you were just zoned out, because the people there are hearing the same old same old, and they're contemplating their next game of *Pokémon Go*? Did you fail to notice that the department was just fine that time you were out for a few months because of major back surgery? All of these kinds of things suggest that a crash course in learning to take the perspective of others, and engaging in active listening during a meeting, might pay dividends. Happily, we now have a substantial body of empirical work showing how it is that meetings can become derailed and how we can run meetings so that they are much more successful in terms of their outcomes. We will focus first on some of the ubiquitous types of cognitive bias that are apparent when people deliberate and discuss things together in a group context. Then, we will focus on how status in groups affects how we behave in those groups. Along the way we will learn that the skill of 'active listening' and perspective taking pays great dividends for both the chairing of successful meetings and also successful leadership.

How Groups Make Poor and Disastrous Decisions

When thinking about the deliberative processes that group meetings are called for, the best practice might be to think of a group meeting, at least in its early stages, as being analogous to the resting state network, or default mode network of the brain, whose job, in part at least, is to push or surface new ideas into consciousness; the consciousness here being a collective and trans-active one, with the social functions of consciousness being key. One answer to the question of why we are conscious arises from thinking about social life and group life. Consciousness is fundamental as far as our social lives are concerned—the best parties do not happen while we are asleep! Consciousness therefore has an important social transaction function—one that extends far beyond what happens within the hidden recesses of a single individual's brain. It is reasonable to argue that without conscious experience, and the capacity to represent and comprehend the internal mental worlds of others, that our rich social world would not exist.

Poor Decisions by Groups

History is replete with examples of poor decisions taken by groups. These can run from bad decisions over acts of war that sink whole countries to product launches that sink companies. Poor decision-making can, of course, be of a lesser level, as Adam Smith famously put it: 'There's a great deal of ruin in a nation', meaning that nations can continue to function below par as a result of poor decision-making, for very considerable periods of time, while they quietly squander their accumulated capital of the ages. In Western Europe, for example, Italy provides a sad example of this: a country that, because of its idiosyncratic decision-making processes, is unable to reform itself, and at the same time has generated near-zero levels of economic growth over a 30-year period, while simultaneously being capable of producing world-class organisations that dominate the fashion, motor and food industries. That there is a lot of ruin in nations is equally true of organisations. Organisations can run suboptimally because of their poor procedures and processes, with meetings providing a key pinch-point at which these poor procedures and processes become visible. Organisational and institutional inertia, however, may strongly militate against badly needed organisational change. Cass Sunstein and Reid Hastie, in their remarkable book '*Wiser: getting beyond groupthink to make groups smarter*' (2015), analyse in detail the cognitive processes and behavioural problems that can cause organisations trouble with regard to the deliberative processes that the organisations use in order to develop some product or process, or indeed simply to take a decision. The key problem that bedevils deliberative processes at all levels of organisations is one of accessing, integrating and acting upon critical hidden information that may be held by members of the deliberative group, or indeed held by people who should be members of that group, but for whatever reason are not. Groups lacking cognitive diversity fail at vital problem-solving tasks and are subject to a whole variety of processes that amplify faulty decision-making. The consequences of this can be disastrous. These can be straightforward, from product launches failing terribly, which sink a company; from product rebranding, which can be undertaken for little better than vanity reasons, which in turn can cause catastrophic decline in sales. Kellogg's, the cereal company, discovered this in 1998, when they renamed their very successful cereal product 'Coco Pops' as 'Choco Krispies' in the UK. Sales were affected, consumers complained, and Kellogg's had to quickly rename 'Choco Krisps', in the guise of a consumer preference competition, as Coco Pops again in 1999.

Sunstein and Hastie (pp. 23–24) suggest groups may encounter four problems when they are engaged in deliberative processes. First, they might not correct errors that particular individuals (who may be central, cognitively or in status terms) to the group's functioning, leading to the amplification of the error by a group. Second, there can be cascade effects, where the initial speaker or speakers create a follower effect, where those that follow afterwards take their lead and do not deviate from it. Third, groups can become substantially more polarised than even the most extreme member of their groups, leading them to take risks or to have beliefs that are substantially at variance with reality. Finally, group discussions or deliberative discussions have a very strong tendency to engage in discussing information that is already known and shared by most or all of the members of the group, information that Sunstein and Hastie characterise as knowledge that 'everyone knows already'. The error here, of course, is to engage in a discussion that supports or reinforces a pre-existing confirmation bias, because, of course, this is more intrinsically rewarding than engaging in a probing discussion that seeks the limits of what is known or that focuses on areas of error. Additional variables may also come into play that support these four fundamental problems. People in groups may engage in acts of self-silencing, whereby they do not volunteer critical information because of problems revolving around social incentives or informational signals. Social incentives can be quickly and clearly understood: this is where, for reasons of self-preservation, self-interest or fear of the group chair, the possessor of important information judges that the cost or consequence of speaking up outweighs the benefit. One solution here, of course, is to solicit opinions in advance and circulate these opinions anonymously ahead of time, in other words, having an information-gathering phase distinct from a deliberation phase. Information signals are somewhat more complex. These revolve around the individual in a group context coming to judge that their knowledge is in some way defective, even if in fact their knowledge is correct.

Social Conformity in Groups

The classic example arises from the Solomon Asch studies of social conformity originally conducted in the 1950s. Asch was interested to understand the dynamics of what it is makes people conform to judgements in a group context, which are clearly at variance with reality. His experimental paradigm was deceptively simple and is easy to replicate. A group of individuals are brought to a conference table. One is a stooge; the other are confederates. The stooge is led to believe that this is the first time the confederates and the stooge have met each other. They are told by the experimenter that they are engaged in a simple task to do with visual perception. A series of cards are then displayed to the room. These cards have lines drawn on them, two of which are the same, the third of which may or may not be different. Each person presents their judgement in turn, with the stooge usually being second last or last. On the first couple of passes, the clearly different line (the shorter or longer line) is adjudged to be different from the two comparison lines. And then, after these few passes, the judgements start to change and the confederates give a line length judgement, clearly at variance with reality. They do this slowly and carefully and deliberately in sequence, and the stooge is left in the uncomfortable position of possibly having to state something in public that he knows to be incorrect, namely that the shorter or longer line is identical in length to the other two lines. Most people, most of the time, find this situation quite stressful, and they start to doubt their own judgement and defer to the judgement of the group.

So what happens with these individuals? Are they simply overtly denying the covert and correct judgement of their senses, or is it that they are coming to see the incorrect line as the same length as the result of the group or peer pressure that they have been exposed to? The answer, sadly, appears to be the latter. In people who are susceptible to the Asch effect, brain-imaging experiments conducted by Gregory Berns and his colleagues (2005) have found that there is a modification in the activity of the visual perceptual areas of the brain during these socially mediated perceptual judgement tasks. In other words, people come quickly to disbelieve the evidence of their own senses, and their senses in turn start to conform to what it is that the group sees, not what they individually see. This effect also turns out to be true of memory, as has been demonstrated by Ray Dolan and his colleagues. They have found that when people are misled during recall by the statements of group members who say they recall information that was not, in fact, present during the original learning experience, those who behaviourally show false recall also show modification of the brain circuits that support memory, relative to those who have not had false recall.

These experiments demonstrate that there are powerful psychological and neural mechanisms at work here. It may in fact be reasonable for an individual to doubt the evidence of his or her own eyes, or indeed the lack of evidence of his or her own eyes. Being a member of a group that might be stalked by a predator doesn't leave you with much time to make a judgement: if someone shouts 'There's a tiger' and you think it's a bush, then you may end up as a tasty meal, whereas your group members, which may include those who decided that, actually, they don't care whether it's a bush or a tiger, they're going to run because they don't have the time to make such a judgement, will have survived. The problem, of course, is that these socially mediated transactive processes exert powerful effects in domains for which they never evolved and in which we routinely find ourselves in modern life.

Is the news all bad with regard to group deliberation or group discussions? The answer is, of course, no. Sunstein and Hastie (pp. 25–26) emphasise that groups can and do work exceptionally well together, and when they do work very well together, some remarkable effects start to appear in the group. They emphasise three in particular. The first is that a group that works well, which surfaces the relevant and necessary information and is capable of integrating it and acting upon it, work at the level of their best members, not at the level of the average of their members of or their worst members. Such groups are capable of solving difficult problems with what may be fuzzy or ill-defined solutions, but for which solutions are required quickly. A key example, of course, is the rapid response of the healthcare company Johnson & Johnson to the Tylenol controversy that engulfed it several decades ago. In this case, Johnson & Johnson quickly and effectively took ownership of the problem, removed the product that had been tampered with from the shelves, gave refunds and put in place tamper-proof bottles to replace the old-style bottles. As a result, Tylenol continues to be a very effective and prominent brand name in over-the-counter medication. A dark version of effective group deliberation revolves around how well the tobacco industry fought over a period of decades against the evidence provided by public health doctors and others, showing that smoking has catastrophic effects on human health and exacerbates disease. To this day, the tobacco industry has fought very effectively to forestall regulatory change that would damage what is for them a very powerfully incentivised product: one that causes addiction and that has been a public health catastrophe, with all that that entails.

Sunstein and Hastie also emphasise that groups, if they are working correctly and properly, can aggregate information in new and creative ways as a result of an iterative process of discussion and idea testing within groups. Finally, they also suggest that very effective groups generate powerful synergies where new and non-obvious solutions to difficult problems are devised and pursued vigorously. A good example of this kind of thinking has occurred in the aviation industry. A very successful Irish aviation company, Ryanair, originally started life as a full service airline, competing with the historic flag-carriers of Aer Lingus and British Airways, on a very limited number of routes between Ireland and the UK. The company was losing tremendous amounts of money attempting to compete with what were country flagship airlines. Unable to compete, and unwilling to simply go bankrupt, Ryanair decided to invert their business model and become a low-cost airline, with all of the frills removed. Three decades, 100 million passengers per year, and hundreds of millions in euros of profit every year, the rest is history. Other low cost airlines have also come into the market, and the air transport industry was decisively changed as a result. The decision to make this change, and to change the internal policies to make it happen, resulted from two processes: an information gathering one, conducted in the USA, where Southwest Airlines (the original low-cost airline) was studied closely as a model. The second was a deliberative process in Ryanair itself, which considered a number of different possibilities, which included closing the airline. In the end, the low-cost model was chosen, and air travel in Europe was altered dramatically.

Curing the Problems of Deliberative Groups

Sunstein and Hastie make a number of suggestions for curing some of the problems of deliberative groups. There are others available from a consideration of the relevant literature as well. Here are a couple of suggestions. First, be very clear about the purpose of the group. Is it merely an information transmission group, or is it an information-gathering group as well? In other words is the group simply being provided information, but substantive discussion is not required of it? It is very important to ensure that the purpose of the group and the economic cost of assembling that group are considered very carefully. Having figured this absolutely central and elemental problem out, it then may be appropriate to consider the processes and procedures that are to be adopted, depending on the type of problem that the group has to solve. If group problems revolve around large strategic issues that will set the tone and direction for the organisation over a coming period of time, then an appropriate deliberative checklist needs to be established for the group. In essence, the purpose of the checklist is to ensure that during the course of deliberation, the group does not rely simply on the hope that individuals will have sudden insight, that individuals do not suffer from cognitive fatigue, variations in cognitive load or whatever. Next, especially for larger strategic issues, the group should separate information-gathering and solution-generating as much as is possible from decision-making processes. In fact, Sunstein and Hastie suggest that the second stage should be one where senior individuals not normally involved in the group's work should be brought in to test and provide feedback on the various ideas provided by the group from its solution-generation and information-gathering phase.

Central to optimal group functioning is the idea that cognitive diversity is important and necessary for the group to work at its most effective. Diversity in what each individual brings cognitively to the table allows the group to use individual expertise that each individual may possess and to use it in a way that is most effective for generating the best solution for the problem at hand. For difficult, contentious or simply very important strategic decisions, there must be a formal process that allows all information possessed by all of the members to be brought to the table. There are many ways of ensuring that this can happen, from simple emails to a nominated individual who provides all the information suggested by the group, back to the group, in an anonymous fashion, or whatever. The key thing here, though, is that the chair of the group, the person who will be running the meeting, in turn is open to generating the best solution, which may differ from their preferred solution. Ego might be a problem here. Finally, in the information-gathering stage, having empirical information in the form of data that allow you to benchmark the quality of the decision or decisions that need to be made, should also be made. In other words, the metrics by which you can measure outcomes need to be stated, and these in turn can be used to anchor the discussion. These need to be reliable; they need to be realistic, and in certain cases, may not exist at all. For the launch of an entirely new product or category of product, no such information may be available, but the necessity for the product might be available through other means. A simple example is to go back to the early days of the World Wide Web. It was possible in the early 1990s, over the course of a day, to visit all of the websites that existed on the then internet, using a simple browser such as Mosaic. As the internet grew and evolved, remembering which website to go to was ever more of a problem, and finding which website to go to was also a problem. Lists or spread sheets of these websites started to become available, often in an online fashion, and thus the problem of search was born: an entirely new problem, driven by cognitive overload on the internet, and which required a rapid solution. The solution that most people now use ultimately derives from a slightly obscure application of set theory in mathematics, but which gave us, by certain counts, the world's most valuable company, namely Google (or Alphabet, as the overall holding company is known).

One final process might need to be added, and this is the process known as a 'premortem'. This is where, having arrived at the solution or strategy, a fresh team or a reconstituted version of the current team is asked to figure out why, if this product fails, why it has failed. And working through such a counterintuitive solution space might be very valuable indeed, because it forces you to ask questions that otherwise one might prefer to leave unasked.

Is our bank sufficiently capitalised? What can we do to prevent a run on our capital? Are we overleveraged? Should we, as a bank (in 2006), jump whole-heartedly into the mortgage market—a market that blew up spectacularly two years later and the fallout from which we are still attempting to adjust? Should we, as a car manufacturer, deliberately massage the safety of our vehicles to sell more products? What will we do if we are found out? Should we as a pharmaceutical manufacturer close arms of clinical trials that are costing huge sums of money, but which are ones in which we as a corporation are heavily invested? These kinds of latter decisions involve recognising that sunk costs are just that—they are gone, and the decision that needs to be made now, needs to be made, as the economists put it, at the margin. The past is just that, past. The money spent is just that, spent. A vital question then is: what should we do now? This is a particularly difficult problem for groups to get beyond—the idea that sunk costs can be recovered (the 'sunk cost' fallacy). Someone needs to be empowered to say 'don't throw good money after bad'. And meetings need to have stop mechanisms for decisions—just as much they need go decisions. Our brains are biased for action—and, paradoxically, sometimes inaction might just be the best course of action.

Optimally Designing Groups and High-Performance Teams

There has been much debate recently about the related issues of designing groups and high-performance teams to ensure that they function optimally, and avoid the dangers of groupthink, and the myriad other cognitive biases that afflict individual and group decision-making. The design of groups and feedback to individuals within groups can dramatically impair or enhance individual and group performance. One important study (Kishida and colleagues 2012) shows that feedback regarding IQ in a group context can dramatically *diminish* IQ and individual performance on tasks performed in the group. Furthermore, activity changes are seen in brain areas that support memory and executive function. In other words, the how, where, what and why of feedback provided to individuals while in a group can dramatically reduce their performance. Managers and leaders need to consider very carefully indeed how to give feedback. These data might explain why 'stack-ranking' regimes are profoundly demotivating and destructive. A complementary study shows that well-designed groups have a collective intelligence that rises above what you predict from the sum of individual intelligences (Woolley et al. 2010). The key variables are for group designs are: the average social sensitivity of group members, the equality in distribution of conversational turn taking and the proportion of females in the group.

Exercise

1. Think of the worst meeting or series of meeting that you have ever attended. Write down, in short words and phrases, why it was so bad. How could it have been changed?
2. Think of the best meeting or series of meeting that you have ever attended. Write down, in short words and phrases, why it was so good. How could it have been changed?
3. Take the case study that was used to introduce this book. How, if you were Tom Spengler, and knowing what you know happened, would you have set up the group deliberation processes to ensure a different, and perhaps, better outcome. How would you define better—in *measurable* ways?
4. You have a complex decision to make: you have what looks like a good outcome from a small-scale clinical trial involving about 80 patients who were trialled on a new drug for Alzheimer's disease. You know that at least 100 candidate drugs have failed in the past and the likely cost of a full-scale clinical trial will be at least in the £100–200 million range. What deliberative processes do you put in place to help the decision about what to do next?
5. You are the new CEO of a failing tech company with a high-recognition product, poor innovation and company culture that is too indecisive and riven with in-fighting. What do you do to turn things around?

Further Reading

Berns GS, Chappelow J, Zink CF, Pagnoni G, Martin-Skurski ME, Richards J (2005) Neurobiological correlates of social conformity and independence during mental rotation. Biol Psychiatry, 58:245–253.
Kishida KT, Yang D, Quartz, KH, Quartz SR, Montague PR (2012) Implicit signals in small group settings and their impact on the expression of cognitive

capacity and associated brain responses. Phil.Trans. R. Soc. B, 367(704–716). doi: 10.1098/rstb.2011.0267.

Mankins MC (2014) This weekly meeting took up 300,000 hours a year. Harvard Business Review. Harvard, Boston, MA. https://hbr.org/2014/04/how-a-weekly-meeting-took-up-300000-hours-a-year.

Sunstein C, Hastie R (2015) Wiser: Getting beyond groupthink to make groups smarter. Harvard Business Review Press, Cambridge, MA.

Woolley AW, Chabris CF, Pentland A, Hashmi N, Malone TW (2010) Evidence for a collective intelligence factor in the performance of human groups. Science, 330(686–688). doi: 10.1126/science.1193147.

8

Brain Hygiene, Optimising Expertise and Performance

This chapter explores how to ensure that best performance is achieved during the course of learning.

Expert performance is on-the-job execution to a high standard of the work or task that you are engaged in, by bringing to bear your capacities, abilities, resources and attention to execute the task to a demanding standard. In this chapter I will be examining some of the most important factors associated with on-the-job performance, including learning and memory, and other important factors that underpin these such as sleep, aerobic fitness, self-control, motivation and mind-sets/conscientiousness. First, though, let's undertake a thought experiment. I want you to imagine that you're a taxi driver in London, one of the world's oldest, largest and complex cities. A city in a constant state of flux with more languages in use than almost anywhere else on the planet; it is Europe's largest city, with a population not far off nine million people. You've been driving this city for years; you are not allowed to rely on sat-nav systems, unlike other drivers. To qualify as a taxi-driver, you have learned the route between any two points in a city with 25,000 streets in an area of 113 square miles. What effect does this have on your brain? Well, we can think of the brain as muscle—it develops as a result of training or cognitive exercise—the 'use it or lose it' principle. In a now famous set of studies of taxi-drivers, Eleanor Maguire and her colleagues (2000) studied spatial memory in expert and novice London taxi-drivers. Expert taxi-drivers were found to have larger right hippocampi than novices and controls. There are two possibilities: these individuals became taxi-drivers because of their enlarged hippocampi *or* the hippocampus *grew* because

© The Author(s) 2018
S. O'Mara, *A Brain for Business – A Brain for Life*, The Neuroscience of Business, https://doi.org/10.1007/978-3-319-49154-7_8

of repeated learning and exposure to routes. The flipside of this plasticity is that cells and connections may atrophy and die from *lack of use*, hence the drive to keep the mind active into old age, to prevent cognitive deterioration like Alzheimer's disease and dementia. The lesson is clear: a healthy mind and body requires activity.

Brain Hygiene, Sitting and Exercise

A question is floating around the blogosphere: *is sitting the new smoking?* A theme of this book is that aerobic exercise is good for the brain in a whole variety of direct and indirect ways. We know with certainty now that regular aerobic exercise is absolutely vital for good heart health. Less widely appreciated is the fact that the heart is, of course, directly connected with the brain, and the quality of blood flow through the brain has a dramatic effect on brain function. This manifests itself in a variety of ways. These include what appear to be decreased rates of dementia among those who are aerobically fit. Humans are not designed to spend long hours sitting around. Our metabolic rates rise substantially when we make a simple transition from sitting to standing. Our (orthostatic) blood pressure also changes when shifting from sitting to standing. Humans as a species have migrated to every geographic locale on the planet, from the Arctic to the Antarctic. No other species has done this. We haven't done this because we are the fastest runners, or the fastest at flying, or because we are the fastest at crawling. What we excel at is walking very long distances over long periods of time. It should be no surprise that walking in nature and walking generally is a remarkably good relaxant, a remarkably good anti-stress treatment and even one of the very best treatments for lower back pain (which may of course arise from excessive periods remaining seated). Modern work practices, where we spend long hours seated facing computer screens or in meetings, need simple but effective behavioural design changes. These changes manifest themselves in all sorts of other positive ways, from an enhancement of subjective wellbeing in staff to increased productivity.

Anecdotal evidence suggests that meetings conducted while walking or standing tend to be over more quickly and to be more to the point than the traditional seated format. There is another important possibility, which has as yet gone unrecognised in the literature. Many meetings are conducted, for reasons of architectural convenience, around a table where participants can focus on the eye position and eye gaze of others. We human primates, in fact, have a very elaborate eye positioning system in the brain (the 'oculomotor' system), which is coupled with another system designed to judge the movements of others, including the eye movements of others (the 'mirror neuron' system). Humans famously engage in displays of aggression or hostility by means of an unwavering gaze of the eyes. A walking meeting offers the chance to break this script. When walking, eye movements are directed frontally and in a common direction, and lateral movements are much less frequent and are signalled usually by a head movement. A walking meeting, therefore, offers an important opportunity to conduct a short, focused discussion around what might be a contentious or difficult issue, with the latent cues that exacerbate hostility and anger (in particular, eye gaze and fixation) removed. Furthermore, because walking is conducted typically in outdoor settings, the temptation to violate social norms through shouting is reduced, because of the unwanted attention that raised voices will bring to the group. It may well be that a walking meeting of this type will only walk best where a small number of participants are involved. An important literature suggests that walking or mobility also contributes to positive mental health in a variety of ways. Epidemiologically, those who walk more regularly tend to be less prone to depression, fear and anxiety disorders. There is also an important set of suggestions in the literature that walking fosters creativity. It is certainly the case that many creative artists extol the benefits of walking for their subsequent work. Many writers certainly claim this. Walking is a central feature of the creative output of the travel writer and historian of science, Bill Bryson, who has discussed walking in many of his popular books. We know that during walking or locomotion that the activity of a wide variety of brain areas becomes activated and indeed synchronised in time (technically, this is most easily demonstrated in the theta rhythm, which is a predominant feature of brain activity during locomotion). It is not too far of a stretch to suggest that walking, by virtue of its generalised effects on brain function, its activation of widespread and disparate brain areas, and by virtue of its tapping into mechanisms associated with relaxation, is a positive boon to creativity and enhancing subjective well-being.

Redesigning workplaces to facilitate walking and movement more generally should enhance productivity. In a clever recent study, Nisbet and Zelenski (2011) examined the effect of people undertaking walks where they are exposed to nature, versus walking in an enclosed environment. Carleton University, Ontario, is subject to extremes of weather. A substantial fraction of the large campus is connected via a system of extended underground tunnels. They investigated (150 participants; 18–48 years) the effect of walking between two locations on the campus: either through an underground tunnel or over ground past an urban space with trees and other features of the natural environment. Participants underestimated dramatically the likely hedonic benefit of undertaking a 17-minute walk outdoors versus a walk indoors. They also found that the effect of the walk itself on affect, or mood, was very substantial (an improvement in score of one third) relative to individuals who undertook a walk indoors. Thus, activity in an outdoor setting is an important and positive moderating variable on individual mood, independent of its effects on cognition. Walking improves how you feel, but walkers underestimate how much walking in nature is likely to make them feel. The walk along the riverbank with plenty of exposure to nature was rated as much more mood enhancing than the walk through the long, enclosed tunnel. In other words, physical activity outdoors is, to some extent, a simple behavioural antidepressant. Mere exposure, on an intermittent basis, to nature has a strong, sustained effect on mood. Behavioural design measures for buildings and for cities could easily take account of factors like this. It has recently been found, for example, that when controlling for income, socioeconomic status and a whole host of other variables, urban areas that tend to have many trees present and green space available have lesser rates of crime compared with areas that do not.

Learning and Memory: The Basis of Expert Performance

Imagine you are sitting at your desk, thinking about what it is that you have to do. This is an example of 'prospective memory', a type of memory focused on remembering your future intentions, rather than the focusing on past acts. Prospective memory includes specific behavioural plans to be implemented. Such plans, ideally, should be written down because, as we are all well aware, plans can be easily and quickly forgotten when the next interruption occurs. As you sit there, an email pops up requesting information on a file on your laptop. You think about this for a moment, and you recall exactly what is required—this is an example of 'declarative' memory, a fact or an event that you can recall and state out loud. Next, somebody rings you, calls out their awkward Skype name, which, as you write it down, you can feel it disappearing, but you hold it in your head for a short period of time, perhaps one to two seconds. This is rehearsed through what is sometimes referred to as the 'phonological loop', a part of the memory system that is designed to hold short sounds and phrases for very short durations of time. Even with this little thumbnail sketch, it should be apparent that our memory is amazing. To take a slightly different and very prosaic example, if I ask you your name, you can tell me, and you can tell me quickly and rapidly. Yet, you learned your name before you could speak, sometime in the first two or three months after birth, and barring accidents, you will know your name perhaps eight or nine decades later, right up to, or at least close to the point of death. This is a remarkable feat of memory for our brains to perform, particularly given the huge changes that a brain goes through during this period of time. It grows, it develops, it is educated over a very long period of time, it matures, and it also ages. How can a brain do this? And knowing how a brain can do this, can we improve our performance on learning and memory tasks?

We now have some reasonable first principle answers that allow us to explain how a brain can recall like this. But before we explore these, first, take out a sheet of paper, and from memory, try to perform each of the following tasks:

First, think about what is possibly the most famous portrait painting in the world—Leonardo da Vinci's 'Mona Lisa'. Draw a simple rectangle in portrait format, and now try and remember which direction her head faces. Is it to the left as you look at it or is it to the right?

Second, we've all heard of Steve Jobs and Apple computers, which have been a part of personal computing for more than 30 years, and their other products such as the iPhone are ubiquitous. Now, think, how many times have you seen the Apple logo? It must be hundreds, if not thousands of times. Try and sketch the logo from memory, and after you've done that, on a scale of one to ten, rate how confident you are in your recall and how accurate you think your picture is.

Third, you handle money fairly regularly. Think, when was the last time you handled a 20 pound or a 20 euro note? It might have been this morning. Now, describe the note, front and back. Award yourself no points for saying it has the number 20 on it, and it has a currency unit represented on it. What size is it? What colour is it? What images are present on it?

Fourth, like many people, you may have a very regular route to work. Perhaps you take the same train or bus every day, or perhaps you drive the same route every day, something you experience for, say, 30, 45 minutes. Now, think about your commute last Thursday week. Don't look at your diary; just think about the commute. What can you recall about it? Unless something exceptional occurred, you won't recall anything.

Fifth, those who were alive at the time, and old enough, will recall September 11, 2001. Your memory may have faded a bit, but images of that day will pretty readily come to mind. Now, try and recall September 11, 2004. Hard, isn't it? There's nothing distinctive about that day.

Now, go check your answers. You can look up the Mona Lisa and the Apple logo quickly and easily. You may even carry an iPhone, which will allow you to do both of these at once. You can repeat tests like this quickly for many other items that we encounter on a daily basis. How many keys are in your key ring? Most people can't give an exact answer: they give an estimate. How many trees line your road? Again, you'll give an estimate, which is unlikely to be the precise and accurate number, despite the fact that you might have walked past every single one of these trees for the past half-decade or more. The uncertainty you felt doing these tests should be a good reminder of the fallibility of the operations of your own memory.

The key point is: just because something feels familiar, doesn't mean that you've learned anything meaningful about whatever that 'something' is.

Let's take a different example. Can you ride a bicycle? Almost certainly. Most people learn this skill somewhat painfully in their middle childhood years, and with a little practice, perhaps a wobble or two, can resume cycling even after intervals of 10 or 20 years. Now, describe how it is that you cycle a bicycle to somebody else. Not easy, is it? It is more or less useless to say to somebody who has never cycled a bicycle that what you have to do is sit up on the saddle, get yourself into dynamic equilibrium with the environment and apply a force of so many Newtons to the pedals, while stabilising your trajectory with your hands on the handlebars. This is an example of a motor or procedural skill, one that was acquired through practice, and the specifics of which are difficult, if not impossible to describe in words to someone else. Note, this is not the same thing as being able to tell someone else you can cycle a bike. It is the actual doing that is at hand here.

The key point here is this: mere exposure to information does not ensure learning, nor does exposing someone to information change their behaviour. If this were true, that mere exposure to information affected behaviour profoundly, public health campaigns against smoking would meet great success and little resistance. In fact, the formation of new habits can be, especially for adults, very difficult. Lally and colleagues (2010) tracked how long it took for a new health behaviour to become a habit. Examples of a new health behaviour might be doing 50 sit ups after your morning coffee, taking a brisk ten-minute walk directly after breakfast or engaging in 15 minutes of exercise prior to eating dinner in the evening. The authors summarised their study (somewhat disheartingly) as follows: 'The time it took participants to reach 95% if their asymptote of automaticity ranged from 18 to 254 days.' So, a new habit, one that can promote health, can take up to two-thirds of a year before that habit becomes one that is automatic. One small piece of good news from the study was that missing the new behaviour on the odd occasion did not affect the speed with which the behaviour itself becomes automatic, putting to bed the old idea that interruptions during habit formation can be fatal to new habit formation.

Your Memory: A Brief User's Guide

We now know, after several decades of painstaking research and patience, in normal human volunteers and in animals, the general shape and operating principles of the memory systems of the brain.

Some important introductory points:

First, memory consists of differing types of memory, operating on different timescales and in different brain systems.
Second, damage to differing brain regions causes reliable changes in memory function.
Third, the brain regions involved in 'declarative' or 'explicit' memory are the hippocampal formation and the anterior thalamus; working memory, sometimes referred to as short-term memory, a number of regions in the frontal lobes; and motor, habit and related forms of memory involve brain regions such as the striatum and the cerebellum.
Finally, memory itself results almost certainly from changes in the strength of connections between individual brain cells.

When we consider learning in its most abstract form, we can think of it as occurring in three related phases. The first is *encoding*, the second is *consolidation*, and the third is *retrieval*. Encoding refers to how, for example, marks on a page (letters, words) get somehow translated by cells in the retina and then turned into items, events or behaviours that can be recalled at some other point. The storage of those items, events and behaviours is referred to as consolidation, which is the modification, over short or long scales, of activity within the brain to support memory. Finally, retrieval is the pulling out or accessing of previously learned information. Brown et al. (2014) offer an especially accessible and important treatment of the science of learning and memory, and their book is highly recommended as further reading.

How Well Do You Understand the Operations Underpinning Your Own Memory?

If you watch students trying to learn new material, or watch yourself when you're trying to understand new material, for example, the latest consolidated companies act, or the new regulations that govern the accounting rules and principles for the depreciation of offshore capital investment, you will notice that you underline, highlight and repeatedly reread the passages in question. You may even make notes in those passages, and then you refer to those passages again and you refer to the notes again. In other words, you haven't actually learned the material itself in its totality—what you've actually done is learned where to find the answer to the question that may present itself in the course of your professional work actually is rather than the material itself. This is perfectly reasonable if you are going to be sitting in an office with the time to engage in deliberation and research. It won't work, of course, in a high-pressure environment where answers are required quickly, and the answers themselves must be cogent and to the point. Learners focus on encoding for multiple reasons. It feels active, it feels like you are doing something, the marking of a text with a highlighter or post-its allows you to get some mental map of the text, and it feels somewhat effortful. Learners possibly do this also because they see other learners engaging in this behaviour. The question actually is, do learners have an accurate insight into how it is that they can learn, and are they learning information in a way that allows them to use that information quickly and easily, at some other time? The short answer is no. A focus on encoding is actually not the best way to engage in learning. Marking texts as well as rehearsing the words in that text is a poor learning strategy, especially if you have limited time available. How you go about learning also affects consolidation. Additionally, the rate at which learners attempt to learn new information and the number of interpolated sleep/wake cycles prior to recall have a profound effect on learning itself. Finally, *retrieval* is affected by *lack of retrieval* (that sounds like a paradox, and it is).

Let's explain this a little bit further. Imagine you are learning a new language (a 600-page undergraduate textbook in neuroscience may have an average of five new technical terms on every page. That's 3,000 words to be learned, which is, effectively learning a new language. Now, imagine you are learning a new language such as French or Italian. You will spend most of your time attempting to retrieve the correct words and phrases in the appropriate context while attempting to understand what it is that someone else might be saying to you. Retrieval is actually the key, not encoding, but learners focus on encoding and rarely think about either consolidation or retrieval. Formally, the use of learning strategies that are focused around retrieval rather than encoding is known as 'retrieval practice', and it is probably the most effective or powerful way of actually learning. It involves recalling the test material, or the to-be-learned material, from memory, whether this is words, sentences, ideas, concepts or indeed a sequence of finger movements at a piano key, or the stroke of a golf club. Each act of recall or retrieval causes further elaboration of that memory, through the memory systems of the brain generating further consolidation, in turn making it easier to recall. How many times and in how many places have you had to give your own name when you've been asked for it? Thousands, probably, hence the difficulty of forgetting your own name and the difficulty of learning a new one. On the other hand, much of what we have experienced is evanescent. It disappears, despite the fact that we have experienced it. Think about the last three- or four-hour car journey you have made. You have experienced it, you may have driven the car, you may have used the indicators, you may have used the accelerator, you may have passed somebody out on the motorway, or whatever, but the details are all gone. As Kahneman put it, 'Your experiencing self and your remembering self are strangers to each other'.

How Do You Learn New and Complex Material?

There are a number of principles to use. The first is, after reading through small chunks of the material, write down simple questions and attempt to answer those in bullet-point format, or similarly, before going back to look at the material again. Then, look at it again and correct errors that you may have made in your understanding. Creating very simple quizzes or questions, and testing yourself and attempting to learn by answering those questions, enhances recall dramatically. Repeated bouts of consequence-free questions and answers enhance learning dramatically compared with other methods of learning. Combining this method with another note-taking method that involves not writing out the material that you already just read, but that attempts to understand it conceptually, and elaborates it and relates it to other domains of knowledge that you already have, also enhances learning dramatically and also enhances retrieval of that memory in the appropriate context.

There are other important considerations as well. Imagine you have an important examination next Saturday morning. Should you spend an hour or two per day studying, or should you take Friday off work, stay up all night and attempt to learn all that material for the exam on Saturday morning? The answer should be obvious. A little, often, is much more effectively learned than a lot, infrequently—this is known as the 'spaced practice' effect. Trying to do it all in one go and pulling an 'all-nighter' is a disastrous strategy for at least two reasons: it is not widely appreciated that regular sleep is required for effective learning and memory. Having slept on to be learned material allows you to recall that material much more effectively than would otherwise be the case. Furthermore, sleep deprivation causes degradation in performance on cognitive tasks in direct proportion to the amount of time that you are sleep-deprived. Anyone who has stayed up all night will know this. Anyone who stays up all night repeatedly, or suffers from broken sleep patterns, knows this too, which is why sleep deprivation has been used for generations as a very effective instrument of torture. It is not, however, a useful practice for gathering information.

There are other important means too. If the material to be learned is very complex, for example, if you were learning a complicated and difficult piece of music, a poor strategy is to drill the first section until it is perfect, and then move onto the second section until it is perfect, and then move onto the third section until it is perfect. This actually slows learning and causes a big problem in terms of transitioning from the first section to the second section and from the second section to the third section. A better strategy is to mark the music script up into the appropriate sections and to practice in an interleaved way the different parts, perhaps doing 1, then doing 3, then doing 2, then doing 5 and then doing 1, 2, 3, 4, 5. This is a harder way to learn, but it results in more effective and more efficient consolidation and retrieval of the to-be-learned material.

Learning proceeds best when it is in some sense active, so reflecting upon the to-be-learned material, being able to relate it to other pre-viously learned material, for example, assists in learning. Finally, there are two really important background factors that also enhance learning, which are rarely thought about. The first has already been mentioned above, and that is sleep. Sleep serves a wide variety of important func-tions, but one of the most important functions is that it allows consolidation of learning that has occurred during the day and the elaboration of that material through semantic networks in the brain. This facilitates the use of that material on the next occasion it is to be recalled. Sleep debt builds up over the course of the day, and sleep, when it is of good quality and sufficient duration, is cognitively clarifying and memory enhancing.

Another factor that is also very important for learning and memory is, remarkably enough, aerobic exercise. Multiple studies in animals and in humans have shown that exercise, as an intervention, has marked and profound effects on all aspects of cognitive function, from speed of mental operations, to attention, to memory. Aerobic exercise causes a wide variety of changes in the brain and the body. It enhances the portal circulation of blood to the brain, bringing nutrients and oxygen; it stimulates the production of various molecules that are important for the functioning of brain cells themselves. These molecules can be thought of as being kind of like a fertiliser for individual brain cells, because they support the growth of connections between individual brain cells. Recent studies by, for example, Griffin et al. (2011), show that acute bouts of exercise to exhaustion after learning, using a bicycle in a gym, enhance the kinds of memory supported by the hippocampal formation, and low-impact regular aerobic exercise in elderly adults can actually slow down the rate at which the brain systems that support learning and memory decline and even support some degree of growth in those brain regions (Erikson et al, Erickson et al. 2011). Humans, frankly, are not built for sitting around for extended periods of time. Our offices and our work environments can and should be designed to allow people to stand up and move around regularly during the course of the working day.

Expertise and Expert Performance

Witnessing somebody performing with a high degree of expertise, for example in a sports game or a musical performance, is intrinsically rewarding. However, learning to be an expert, witnessing somebody's stumbling steps along the road to expertise, is not so interesting or rewarding. Expertise and expert performance rely, in very profound ways, on the scaffolding provided by ample prior learning. The more you learn, the easier it is to learn more, because you have the appropriate conceptual scaffolds present to support more learning. In this section, we will deal with expertise and expert performance, drawing on a wide variety of different examples, from skill in chess, to skill in sports.

Expertise and its Relationship to Learning

Humans have a particular propensity to revere people who are seen in some way to be naturally 'gifted': as they put it in sport, people who are 'a natural'. Furthermore, we prefer to see performances from people who are regarded as having achieved a high level of success as arising naturally from underlying gifts, rather than from hard work. This is a peculiar cognitive bias. Nobody comes into the world able to play the piano, or to write, or to read, or to swing a golf club perfectly or give a TED talk. We know in our hearts and souls that apparent giftedness relies on extensive training, yet we choose to ignore the role that such training, such practice, has, in the display of virtuosity. This is a great pity, because, as the science of learning and memory, and of neuroplasticity, demonstrates across many domains, there are 'critical periods' whereby intensive training and effort can make a substantial difference to long-term performance. It is now clear, for example, that few people are born with 'perfect pitch', the ability to effortlessly, it appears, identify musical notes and place them on a scale, and then reproduce them. Anders Ericsson (2016) suggests that estimates of perfect pitch arise naturally, at about one in 10,000 of the population. However, the frequency of perfect pitch increases substantially in 'tonal languages' (such as Vietnamese) compared with other non-tonal languages. Furthermore, perfect pitch can be trained. It can be learned, but it must be trained somewhere between two and six years, when the auditory cortex of the brain is undergoing dramatic remodelling in response to the inputs that it receives from the environment. In other words, this is a critical period for perfect pitch development. A similar rule applies to polyglots—those who can speak multiple languages.

If you wish to acquire another language, to be bilingual or trilingual, the earlier you are exposed to multiple language communities the better, and the earlier you are exposed, the more unaccented by your native tongue will be the other language that you speak, whereas if such language acquisition is left until the onset of adolescence, accent-free language acquisition is almost impossible. Note here also that the children of immigrants learn to speak the language of the language community that they emigrate to in the accent of that language community, if they arrive into that community prior to about seven or eight years of age—again, another critical period is evident. The overall point here is one that has become ever more strengthened by about a century's worth of work in psychology and neuroscience. Ericsson puts it thus: '…dedicated training that drives changes in the brain (and sometimes depending on the ability in the body) that makes it possible for them to do things that they otherwise could not'. Here, while we like to think that genes make a dramatic difference, in general they do not. They make some contribution, but Ericsson's beautiful phrase 'cognitive adaptability' is at the core of all high-level expert performance. Ericsson puts it thus: '…learning now becomes a way of creating abilities rather than of bringing people to the point where they can take advantage of their innate ones' and 'learning isn't a way of reaching one's potential, but rather a way of developing it'. Here is an important point of contact between the mind-set idea generated by Carol Dweck and the idea of expertise as articulated by Ericsson. Dweck gives us a useful and coherent framework for thinking about how behavioural change is possible. Ericsson gives us a useful and coherent methodology by which to effect that behavioural change, and to do so in a high performance way.

What are the key factors to consider? There are some key factors or issues to consider when attempting to establish expert performance, or to improve performance. The first is to establish a current baseline against which future performance can be measured. This baseline should be realistic, and it should in some way be measurable, even if only in some qualitative sense. Second, when establishing one's own baseline, don't look up except as a guide. You need to look down toward your own baseline and seek to incrementally improve relative to that baseline. There is little point, as a fledgling songwriter, looking at Lennon and McCartney, and thinking 'I can never do that', or worse still, 'With a little bit of effort, I can do that'. The next issue to worry about is that of motivation. The important point to note here is that you need to want to do it, and the reward for doing it, ideally, should be intrinsic—to want to do it for the pleasure of doing it for its own sake. As Mallory, the famous mountaineer, put it when asked about the challenge of climbing Everest, 'Why Everest? Because it is there'. The final point is to ensure that the correct kind of motivated effort and practice are aligned, that the principles governing learning and plasticity are, in turn, aligned with motivation.

How Expertise Is Acquired

So, having got the preliminaries out of the way, the universal rule for acquiring expertise is straightforwardly stated. It is sustained, deliberate and purposeful practice, where you want to improve, and you engage in substantial effort to improve. Further, you use mistakes that you make, deliberately, as error-correcting mechanisms to track down deficits in performance. Sports of all types provide a great example of how expertise can develop across the decades. Marathon runners of 100 years ago, with their bare sub-three-hour performances, are running much more slowly than the performers who now run at very close to two hours. Marathon running is not the only example. A recently invented sport, competitive motocross, provides an example of the extreme compression and extension of performance changes that occur. Compare riders of just 10 years ago to riders of today (use YouTube —there are plenty of videos). The range, variety and complexity of their demonstrated moves are astounding now compared to what seemed to be very slow and not especially complex tricks of 10 years ago. And remember, in competitive motocross, the performers are astride motorbikes weighing several hundred kilos, travelling at anything up to 50 or 100 miles per hour. A different but again related example of expertise change seen across populations is provided by the 'Flynn effect': the steady and near-universal improvement seen in IQ scores across all tested populations, since IQ scores were invented. You shouldn't be overly surprised that IQ scores are improving. We are, as a population, taller and healthier than 100 years ago. During normal skill acquisition, most people will tend to practice until they get to a steady-state level of performance. Their performance is pretty good, but it tends not to improve dramatically beyond this particular point. This habitual level of performance, or automatic level of performance, ensures that you stop learning and stop getting better. There are multiple reasons why this might be so, the simplest of which is that the lower level brain systems (typically subcortical systems) that support automatic performance will not be automatically modulated by the higher level systems (typically cortical systems) that will entrain them. Furthermore, as Ericsson puts it '…automated abilities gradually deteriorate in the absence of efforts to improve'. Focusing on incremental changes to steady-state performance is difficult, but it can be done.

What Is Required for Improved Expertise?

Improved expertise and performance require '*purposeful practice*'. This is practice that has several key characteristics (Ericsson 2016). First, purposeful practice has very clearly and well-defined particular goals for practice. These require some form of benchmarks for performance that can be used as the target to improve. There are many of these. In the case of, for example, a musician, it might be an arpeggio played perfectly; for a computer coder, it might be for an app to be smaller and faster, while not losing any functions; for a sports person, it might be something like a relatively error-free swing of the driver, which places the golf ball in the optimum position to allow a clean shot at the tee. Irrespective of the domain, the key point here is that there is a specific benchmark against which progress toward a very well-defined goal can be measured. Associated with a specific or well-defined goal is a set of actual steps that are required to be performed, which allow you to attain the goal. These can be summarised in a series of questions such as 'How, actually, do you do this? What, actually, do you need to do?' In other words, you must have a plan, and you must be able to measure progress towards that plan. Second, purposeful practice has a particular focus, and ironically enough, focus itself is something that can be improved by deliberate, purposeful practice. To improve, you must give the task concentration, you must give it appropriate attention, and you must be aware that to do so is fatiguing. So you need to practice in order to stretch your limits. Paradoxically, as task performance or expertise becomes more automated, it becomes less fatiguing. Thus, there is a sweet spot where focused, concentrated attention stretches performance, induces some degree of cognitive and physical fatigue, but also results in performance increments. Third, this form of practice involves feedback. The feedback can come from at least two sources. The first is simple self-monitoring, where, having established a particular benchmark, for example, the number of successful backhanders returned to a particular sector on a tennis court, or whatever, and practice is oriented deliberately toward improving that. The other form of feedback can come from a third party, a coach or indeed some form of automated monitoring system, but the key thing here is the feedback needs to be quick and reliable, and it should be ideally close in time to actual performance of the task. Finally, this form of practice should always push you out of your comfort zone. Ericsson is emphatic that this is the key component: that you can't be comfortable with your performance and that you must push the limit of what you can do at that moment, when you are practicing. Sometimes, during practice, it may seem that a particular goal is unattainable. If the goal is reasonable and realistic, then this will not be true. The best approach to adopt is to think of this form of practice as also involving some form of creative problem-solving, where if there is difficulty in skill attainment, and then one should try a different approach, changing direction in order to solve the particular pro-blem at hand. Feedback, when it is positive and constructive, is a great source of maintaining positive motivation.

At its core, expertise, whether in physical, competitive sports or in some form of knowledge working (such as coding), involves particular changes in cognitive and neural structures and functions that allow you to avoid the limits of short-term memory and that allow you to deal with masses of information present in the environment quickly and easily. Again, sports provide a very salient example.

In a typical team sport, evenly matched numbers of players play according to some rule set, with the purpose of driving a ball into or over the opponent's goal line. Conditions change dynamically and quickly on the pitch. The job of the players is to read the changes in the play quickly, so that they can direct their own players to gaps if they are defending or to attack gaps if they are in possession of the ball. Games can turn quickly in a matter of a few seconds at most, and skilled players will be able to read player configurations rapidly, allowing them to anticipate the flow of play. The key word here is patterns. Time and again it has been demonstrated that expert performance relies on the ability to extract patterns quickly and easily from the vast array of information that is presented to us. And these patterns must be extracted or, better still, recognised so that the appropriate systems are activated and the direction of play can be anticipated.

Some have argued (for example, Walsh 2016) that sport performance, and in particular team sport performance, represents among the most demanding of human cognitive activities and that they do so in ways that do not necessarily draw on verbal fluency. Indeed, many highly successful sports performers are unfairly derided as inarticulate by individuals who would, of course, be as physically inarticulate as the players are verbally inarticulate, if placed in the same position. These kinds of widespread changes in the structure and function of the brain are directly observable. The canonical example is the change seen in the brains of London taxi drivers (as discussed earlier). To qualify as a taxi-driver in London, it takes usually between two and five years of practice, learning the many thousands of streets and routes that arise in this ancient and extremely crowded city. The longer taxi drivers spend on the job, the larger, typically, is a specialised part of the brain, known as the hippocampus, which supports spatial memory. These changes are not seen in bus drivers who follow largely unvarying routes, which are pre-prescribed for them. So, simple time behind the wheel is not enough to cause changes in the size of the hippocampal formation.

To summarise, therefore, practice must be purposeful, in other words, oriented toward a goal; it must be deliberate; in other words, it must be focused on measurably attaining that goal; and it must be extended through time. There are no naturals who perform at the highest level without years of hidden graft or effort. Ericsson and others, as has been hinted at above, suggest that the key underlying expertise and expert performance is the development of a novel and extended set of mental representations that allow rapid recognition of patterns, and the application of solutions to those patterns in real time. As they say in the USA, 'Nobody cares about a Monday morning quarterback', or as they say in Ireland, nobody cares about the 'hurler on the ditch'. In both cases, these comments refer to the non-player who has had time to think about the course of play after the game has ended and knows better than the team that played just how they should have played. It is performance during the game that is key, not a sudden insight that arises to a non-participant two or three days later. We have mentioned already how retrieval practice is central to learning and memory. Here, again, retrieval practice manifests itself in a very important and reliable way. The more experience that you have of recalling key patterns and the application of solutions to these patterns in a dynamic context, i.e., in real time, the better will be your performance. You may never attain the word level fluency of a child who learns to speak some other language from the cradle, but testing yourself repeatedly with that language will allow you to move from recognising the meaning of words, to recognising the meaning of whole sentences, rapidly and on the fly (i.e., recognising the underlying patterns) and to retrieve the appropriate words and phrases that allow successful performance to occur.

Exercises

1. When did you last go for a walk? Did you go for a walk with someone? In nature? With your phone in your hand?
2. Think about your office. Can you modify it so that you can spend time standing, rather than sitting, during the day?
3. How is your sleep? Do you get enough quality sleep to ensure that consolidation of learning and memory is facilitated?
4. Do you ensure you get a minimum level of activity during the day? At least a few minutes walking every hour?
5. Think about a complex brief you have to master. Instead of reading and re-reading it, how can you facilitate learning by engaging in retrieval practice? Can you ask someone to quiz you on it?
6. Does Tom Spengler exhibit any appropriate brain hygiene practices? How should he change his brain hygiene regime for the better?

Further Reading

Brown PC, Roediger HL, McDaniel MA (2014) Make it stick: The science of successful learning. Harvard University Press, Cambridge, MA.
Erickson KI, Voss MW, Prakash RS, Basak C, Szabo A, Chaddock L, Kim JS, Heo S, Alves H, White SM, Wojcicki TR, Mailey E, Vieira VJ, Martin SA, Pence BD,

Woods JA, McAuley E, Kramer AF (2011) Exercise training increases size of hippocampus and improves memory. Proc Natl Acad Sci., 108(3017–3022). (Epub 2011 Jan 31), 10.1073/pnas.1015950108.

Ericsson KA (2016) Peak: How to master almost anything.Viking, New York.

Griffin EW, Mullally SM, Foley C, Warmington SA, O'Mara SM, Kelly AM (2011) Aerobic exercise selectively improves hippocampal function and increases brain-derived neurotrophic factor in the serum of young adult males. Physiol. Behav., 104:934–941. http://www.sciencedirect.com/science/article/pii/S0031938411003088.

Lally P, Van Jaarsveld CHM, Potts HWW, Wardle J (2010) How are habits formed: modelling habit formation in the real world. Eur. J. Soc. Psychol., 40: 998–1009. doi: 10.1002/ejsp.674.

Maguire EA, Gadian DG, Johnsrude IS, Good CD, Ashburner J, Frackowiak RS, Frith CD (2000) Navigation-related structural change in the hippocampi of taxi drivers. Proc Natl Acad Sci., 97: 4398–4403. doi: 10.1073/pnas.070039597.

Nisbet EK, Zelenski, JM (2011) Underestimating nearby nature: Affective forecasting errors obscure the happy path to sustainability. Psychol. Sci., 22(1101–1106). doi: 10.1177/0956797611418527.

Walsh V, (2016) Is spout the brain's biggest challenge? Current Biology, 24: R859–R860.

9

Stress, Resilience and Positive Brain States

If you are distressed by anything external, the pain is not due to the thing itself but to your own estimate of it; and this you have the power to revoke at any moment. (Marcus Aurelius, Roman Emperor)

First, an experiment: Much of what we know about stress is derived from the study of laboratory animals placed in situations of uncontrollable stress. Place a rat in a small container with a metal mesh floor. Give him occasional, but repeated, mild and inescapable electric shocks. His behaviour will change over time; at first, he will be very active and attempt to escape the container. Eventually he will give up and just sit there—engaging in 'learned helplessness'—in human terms, this is the syndrome characterised by despondency, apathy, anhedonia (or loss of pleasure) and loss of behavioural kinetics that occurs after major life stressors. Next, examine his adrenal glands—these are involved in the secretion of stress hormones, and are located on the kidneys—these will be found to be enlarged. His stomach may show evidence of ulcers, and his immune system may be compromised. Do the experiment again, but place a small piece of wood in the container. Now, the rat will chew the wood; his adrenal glands will be much less enlarged, his stomach will have fewer ulcers, and his immune system will be less compromised. Finally, do the experiment again: place the rat in the container with another rat; shock them as before. Now, they will fight, bite or nip each other and generally be aggressive toward each other; they will not show the learned helplessness characteristic of the lone rat. Now, examine the adrenal glands and stomach; they will appear normal, and the immune system will also appear normal. What lessons can be drawn from this experiment? The simple but trite lesson is that stress is bad for you; more importantly displacing stress via some other behaviour can moderate or reduce the effects of stress entirely - even if you are a laboratory rat.

Popular media suggest that modern society is afflicted by a stress epidemic: a Google search (January 2017) yields 693,000,000 hits for 'stress' and 17,000,000 hits for 'stress epidemic'. Similarly, a Lexis/Nexis search of 'European News Sources' yields 957 news-stories in a *one-week* period on how stress affects the general population. The European Commission has defined work-related stress 'as a pattern of emotional, cognitive, behavioural and physiological reactions to adverse and harmful aspects of work content, work organisation and the working environment...[it is] characterised by high levels of agitation and distress and often feelings of not coping'. Stress is a major cause of neuropsychiatric disorder in contemporary society: stress-related disorders such as anxiety, depression and post-traumatic stress disorder (prevalent after car crashes and physical assaults) are a major burden on the healthcare systems of western societies and diminish individual quality of life. Current EU estimates suggest work-related stress costs over €20 billion p.a. in time and health bills; it is the second most common occupational health problem (after back pain). Stress also damages animal health: substantial crowding among cattle on farms leads to increases in mortality, for example. Campaigns to relieve sources of stress caused by crowding and housing conditions in farm animals are not without foundation.

Stress is a regrettably pervasive phenomenon in modern society. Occupational stress costs organisations and society at large enormous sums of money on an annual basis as well as markedly affecting the health, quality of life and wellbeing of many individuals. A natural question is to focus on how it is that we can learn to cope with stress, what our response to it should be, and how we should adjust both our organisations and our own individual behaviours to better cope with the stressors that we encounter during everyday life. Two key concepts that we're going to deal with in this chapter are that of resilience and that of reserve. These are distinct but related concepts that focus on how it is that we are able to cope with the stressors that are presented to us. One way of thinking about resilience is that it is our capacity to bounce back when confronted with significant adversity, whereas the reserve is possibly better thought of as being more akin to the resources that we can draw on that allow us to do that bounce back. In other words, reserve is what we have 'in the petrol tank', and resilience is our ability to operate the machinery of the car quickly and adaptively to avoid a crash.

Building cognitive and affective resilience and neuroreserve within individuals and teams is a key component of enhancing performance at work. An allied concept to that of resilience is known as stress management—being able to cope and recover from adversity and stress. There has been recent important research on building resilience in individuals working in high-pressure environments (especially in the military, but also in sports). There are object lessons to draw from this kind of work regarding team building and cohesion that translate to other high-pressure environments. Organisations can take steps to institutionalise supporting and developing resilience against the effects of stress. These in turn can pay off in terms of enhanced staff wellbeing.

What Is Stress?

There are many contemporary definitions of stress, but a particularly useful one is provided by David Diamond and Jeansok Kim, where they emphasise that stress consists of three components. The first is heightened excitability or arousal in the brain and body; the second is a perception that present or future events will be unpleasant; the third is a lack of controllability over these events. Consider the responses of two people who are on a rollercoaster ride. One enjoys the rollercoaster enormously, and the other feels sick at the thought of going on the rollercoaster and indeed gets sick as a result of going on the rollercoaster itself. What is the key difference between these two individuals? Well, where stress is concerned, what we would see is both individuals are in a heightened state of arousal, and both individuals would agree that once you're strapped into the trolley car on the rollercoaster, you have no control over what's about to happen to you. At the start of this little experiment it would be very difficult, based just on measures of heart rate, sweating of the palms and stress hormone levels present, to tell which person is going to be the one who will hate the experience and which person will enjoy the experience. The answer here should be clear: it is the second component, how we perceive what it is that is going to happen to us, that makes all the difference. In other words, how we engage in the appraisal of the situation before us is what determines how stressful it is likely to be. One person sees the loop-the-loop as tremendously exciting, and the other person sees the loop-the-loop as a near-death experience. So the evaluation that we place on what is about to happen to us is the key thing in terms of our response to a stressor.

The point here is that our response to stress (the 'stress response') is remarkably similar to a broad range of stressors. And the response itself might be adaptive, because it allows our body and brain to get ready to cope with the stressor that is about to be imposed upon us. The problem arises when the stressor is chronic and inescapable. This may cause problems for general health (in terms of heart problems or immune functions) but also problems for brain function generally, and also for behaviour. And it may well be the case that the stress response itself is more damaging than is the stressor. For example, for someone who is being bullied at work, the anticipation of the conversation, the anticipation of the behaviour of the bully—the shouting, the unreasonableness, the changeability of moods—all of these things may cause a chronic activation of the stress response system, which endures over time, and it is this response that causes problems arising from stress more generally. Damage from the stress response is most likely to arise when the stress itself is unremitting (for example the chronic wear and tear that might be associated with workplace bullying) and an inability to distance oneself from the stressor, and an inability to shut down or quieten down the stress response. It needs to be emphasised, though, that not all stress is bad. In fact, some moderate level of stress that is copeable, and that can be learned from, can be enriching because the stressor can be managed and leads to personal growth and increased effectiveness or enhanced competence at a particular task.

The science of stress is advancing rapidly: it is now known that the stress response is controlled by the hypothalamic-pituitary-adrenal (HPA) axis, a brain circuit shared with all other animals possessing a spinal cord. The HPA axis is also substantially regulated by the hippocampal formation, which is also centrally implicated in the processing of information about memory. Another structure that provides a strong input to the HPA axis is the frontal lobes, where the 'executive functions' of the brain are largely housed. Conscious thinking is also largely housed in and integrated and sustained by the frontal lobes. We regularly encounter stressors in life: Tom, the business executive in the prologue manifests several signs of stress. He feels his heart rate has risen and his mouth is dry; he fiddles and fumbles small objects, showing what is called a 'displacement activity' in an unconscious effort to relieve stress. His words are hesitant and halting and require some conscious effort to utter. His rehearsed lines have seemingly disappeared and he has some transient deficits in what should be a fairly normal act of recall. He experiences a tightening of the chest and, eventually, when subjected to a modern form of predator stress (the assault on his carefully-laid plans and the destruction of his future career), he succumbs to a heart attack.

What underlies these widely experienced phenomena? Behavioural stress caused by uncontrollable but mild electric shocks, by public speaking or even watching certain movies, triggers a reliable and straightforward sequence of events. These start with the evaluation of events in the environment, and these is the key point underlying all of the modern stress literature. The experience of stress is evaluative and perception-based—in other words, it relies on cognition, that is, on what you think, on your mental set, and how you consciously or not frame the events occurring in your environment. It follows therefore that controlling the contents and trajectory of thinking is central to controlling the stress response. There are several techniques from cognitive-behaviour therapy (CBT) that can be used, with practice, that have been shown to be effective at blunting or reducing feelings of stress, without the need for drugs or alcohol.

The Effects of Chronic, Unremitting Stress

The stress response is vital, allowing us to respond rapidly to threat. Physiologically, the release of corticotrophin-releasing hormone (CRH) from the hypothalamus into the portal circulation to the anterior pituitary, which releases adrenocorticotrophic releasing hormone (ACTH) into the bloodstream, causes corticosterone (rat) or cortisol (human) release from the adrenal cortices. ACTH initiates 'fight or flight' responses, mobilises energy stores, decreases reflex thresholds and increases respiratory rate, muscle tension and gastric motility. These effects, if short-lived, are generally positive; pathogenic consequences for cognitive neurobiological functions ensue, however, from elevated and prolonged increases in corticosterone levels.

The literature on stress in humans and animals is enormous. I propose to here provide some exemplar findings rather than a complete summary of the literature. (Readily accessible sources on the effects of chronic and sustained stressors on the human brain and body include O'Mara 2015). In one study, Sonia Lupien and her colleagues (1998) showed that humans who have persistently high levels of the human stress hormone cortisol in their bloodstream have a shrunken (or atrophic) hippocampal formation. What does this mean? The hippocampal formation is a key part of the brain's memory system, and these individuals have, in lockstep with their shrunken hippocampi, deficits in memory performance, something that should be extremely concerning to people whose jobs require them to have quick access to information stored in their long-term memories to perform their jobs appropriately. It can't be argued that these results are merely a sampling error, because we know from work conducted by Dominique de Quervain and colleagues (De Quervain et al. 1998) that volunteers who take hydrocortisone tablets at high doses, under medically controlled conditions, suffer from memory problems. They show about a one-third decrease in their capacity to recall previously learned word lists. Even more impressively, we know from work conducted by Charles A. Morgan III and his colleagues at Yale University Medical School that elite combat soldiers who are selected specifically for their exceptional performance are also subject to the effects of severe stressors. In one particularly important paper, Morgan showed that in combat soldiers drawn from the special forces who were subjected to simulated combat, where live ammunition was used and where they were sleep-deprived, undernourished and dehydrated, that all aspects of both cognitive functioning and all aspects of mood that were measured showed a precipitous decline as a result of the severe stressor that they were exposed to.

Everyday Cognitive Wear and Tear

There are many longitudinal studies underway of cognitive function in adults, where it is assessed regularly through the lifespan. Similarly there are many studies underway that do cross-sectional comparisons of cognitive function in people in their 20s, 30s, all the way up to their 90s. As you might expect, depending on the study population, age, educational attainment level, health status of the individuals involved and a variety of other variables, there are dramatic changes in cognitive function across the life course. For example, in studies by Lusardi and colleagues (Lusardi and Mitchell 2007a,b, c), where the following question was asked 'If the chance of getting a disease is 10%, how many people out of 1,000 would be expected to get the disease?', the fraction of people who answer 100 is nearly 90% at the age of 50, but is down to 50% at the age of 90. In a slightly more complicated question, Lusardi and colleagues asked 'If 5 people all have the winning numbers in the lottery, and the prize is $2 million, how much will each of them get?' The fraction who answer correctly $400,000 at the age of 50 is only about 55%, but shockingly, is less than 10% at the age of 90. In other studies, it seems to be the case that there is a relative stability in many cognitive functions (including inductive reasoning, spatial orientation, numeric ability, visual ability, verbal memory) across the middle years of life with what looks like a fairly precipitous decline once people move into the late 60s or early 70s. One problem with cross-sectional studies is that they are comparing the performance of a 50 year old or a 60 year old or a 70 year old now, to a 20 year old or a 30 year old now, which is of course not the best comparison. A 50 year old now has grown up in a qualitatively different environment to a 50 year old at the turn of the 1900s. A 50 year old at the turn of the 1900s had a rather low life expectancy. A 50 year old in 2016 can, depending on the country they live in, comfortably look forward to 30, perhaps 40 years more life, in the absence of life-limiting illnesses such as cancer or heart disease. Furthermore, a 50 year old now, compared to a 50 year old 100 years ago, will be much better educated, on average; will have grown up in a warm, rather than damp, house, on average; will have been better fed, on average; will have benefited from vaccines, antibiotics, and the whole panoply of modern medicine; in addition to all of the other conveniences that modern life has to offer.

It is also the case that there is enormous variability between individuals. A signal example is to compare two Nobel Prize winners, namely Bertrand Russell and Iris Murdoch. Russell was to win the Nobel Prize for literature, although he was a philosopher, and would in the last 20 years of his life (from his mid-70s) produce approximately 20 books and be involved in the founding of the Campaign for Nuclear Disarmament (CND), amongst many other activities. Iris Murdoch was also to win the Nobel Prize for literature. She was principally a novelist who had been trained in philosophy. She was, sadly, to succumb to Alzheimer's disease and die in her early 70s. The contrast between these two individuals is quite remarkable. We can ask what went wrong with Iris. Equally we can ask what went right with Bertrand. One stance is to focus on the negative problem; the other is to focus on the positive outcome. And we are at last starting to understand the components of resilience and reserve. One controversial but suggestive set of studies by Adam et al. (2007) and Rohwedder and Willis (2010) suggest that the earlier a fraction of the population retires, the greater the decline in cognition that can be observed at a country level in the retired fraction of the population. The data appear to show a reasonably strong relationship between countries like the United States and Sweden, with comparatively later ages of retirement, and greater levels of functioning in that fraction of the population, as compared with other countries such as Spain, France and Belgium, which appear to have slightly lower levels of cognitive function in that early retirement fraction of the population. The key hint here, of course, revolves around the daily challenge and stimulus provided to cognition by continuing to be engaged in the workforce.

Resilience and Reserve: Inoculating Yourself Against the Effects of Toxic Stress

The American Psychological Association defines resilience as 'the process of adapting well in the face of adversity, trauma, tragedy, threats, or even significant sources of stress'. Thus, the emphasis of this widely accepted definition is to suggest that a resilient individual is somebody who has the skill, capacity or ability to avoid mental and physical outcomes that would be in some sense adverse as the result of the toxic stress that they have been exposed to. How widespread is resilience in the population at large? Estimates vary, but depending on the study type, and the toxic stressor that the person has been exposed to, estimates would suggest that anywhere between about a third and two-thirds of individuals are left without any major psychiatric problems as the result of having been exposed to a major traumatic event or series of events. There are important caveats to this suggestion, however, and we will deal with those further on in this chapter. Resilience also appears to be a multi-dimensional phenomenon. People can show great capacity to cope with adversity or stress in one domain of their lives (for example, with regard to academic functioning) but not in other domains (for example, where social functioning or physical function is concerned). Some people can navigate difficult social situations with aplomb, but would be challenged to run a marathon in full battle dress while live ammunition is being fired at them. Others may show quite the reverse capacity. The good news from recent research is that resilience is a learnable 'character skill' that can be acquired, incremented and maintained within the individual. In other words, the level of resilience that you have at a particular point in time is dynamic and subject to development, and it is not simply an enduring and fixed trait of your personality or genetic load.

What Promotes Resilience?

By now, many studies have shown that there are strong positive associations between certain factors and resilience in the individual. These factors are as follows. First, people who are better educated on average tend to have higher levels of resilience, perhaps because they have greater levels of knowledge to draw upon, which allow them to cope with the adverse or toxic stress that they are being exposed to. Second are high levels of social support. People who are deeply embedded within dense social networks and who can easily answer the question 'Who have I got to rely on?' tend to be more resilient, proof of the age-old adage that a burden shared is a burden halved. Third, people who are older tend to show greater levels of resilience than people who are younger. There are many reasons for this possibility. Some revolve around the idea that older people tend to take a more positive view of life; they tend to have great life experience and are able to cope with adversity as a result of that life experience. Fourth, an absence of early life trauma tends to be particularly important, although it is possible to overstate the significance of this factor. It was identified as an important variable in life outcomes for former residents of institutions who were institutionalised in difficult life circumstances early in life and in individuals who have grown up in toxic environments, including difficult inner-city environments, or indeed environments that are subject to the stressors and predation that comes with civil conflicts or war. Fifth, a general optimistic bias in terms of one's psychological orientation towards life, rather than a pessimistic bias, that is to say, individuals who are able to look on the bright side, who look for the silver lining in every cloud, tend to be more resilient than individuals who don't. Finally, specific training, focused on, in particular, how it is that we appraise the situation that we are exposed to, can assist markedly with resilience.

Cognitive Flexibility, Need for Control, and Post-Traumatic Growth

Cognitive flexibility and the need for control really come down to the answers that you would give to the following question. How open to learning, to novel experience and change are you? The socially desirable thing to say, of course, is that you're very open to learning, that you're comfortable with change and that you're happy to engage in new experiences. However, an honest answer to the differing dimensions of this question might throw up a very different set of conclusions. Are you happy when your business requires you to learn new processes and procedures? Are you able to adapt quickly and appreciate the need for a new form of organisation within your business? Do you feel that if your role is changed that this involves some loss of control, and this loss of control is in some way very unpleasant? Post-traumatic growth is a separate concept, and this is really the ability to profit from an unpleasant, stressful or adverse experience.

Control, as a psychological concept, involves several related concepts. The first is how you perceive your ability to handle the challenges of life (how self-confident you are about your ability to manage things). Second, it involves understanding and recognising that certain factors in one's life are external, and how you characteristically respond to these external changes is really the key. This is captured in a concept known as 'locus of control', which refers to the idea that we are all capable of interpreting what happens to us as deriving from our own actions or as visited upon us by an uncaring external world. Locus of control is captured in questions like the following. Do you agree, don't know or disagree with the following contentions? 'Success in life is pretty much determined by forces outside our control.' 'What happens in my life is often beyond my control.' What we see when we look at population responses to questions like this is a really very marked, age-related, income-related and country-related responding. One survey [xx get citation] suggests, for example, that people in the USA are most likely to disagree with the contention that success in life is determined by forces beyond the control of the individual, whereas individuals in Bangladesh are most likely to agree with that contention. When you look at age as a factor, you find that people in their mid-20s to mid-30s are most likely to disagree with the idea that what happens in their lives is beyond their control, whereas people in their early 60s to mid-70s are much less likely to disagree with that contention. A similar pattern is seen in respect to income. People who have low incomes tend to be more willing to agree with the contention that what happens in their lives is beyond their control, whereas people with high incomes (unsurprisingly) are least likely to agree with this contention.

When we look at the workplace, what we see is that people who have greater control and greater autonomy over their work tend to suffer lesser levels of job-related stress. This can be demonstrated in a wide variety of ways. Steptoe and colleagues (2004), for example, showed that people at work who can decide when they take a break have lower levels of ambulatory blood pressure than people who are not allowed control over things like when they can take a break. There is an important lesson for employers here, which is that humans are not machines and our bodies are not machines. Humans need care, they need maintenance, and they need some degree of control over their circumstances to perform optimally. Scheduled and timetabled toilet breaks, for example, for somebody who may have stomach problems would be seen to be extremely aversive and unpleasant. Another way of engaging in control has already been mentioned, namely cognitive reappraisal (Seligman 1991). Cognitive reappraisal refers to how it is that we think about what is happening to us and how we reframe the events in our lives so that we can find some form of meaning or some positivity in a crisis (for example, reframing a crisis as some form of opportunity: to engage in a new business, to develop new markets, or simply to think about other ways of doing what you do). A great example is how Marvel Comics reengineered themselves away from being the writers of comic books to being an entertainment company. Marvel as a comic book enterprise would now be bankrupt if they had persisted with their old business model when the internet changed everything utterly. When they reframed themselves as an entertainment company with a rich stream of characters and stories to mine, which in the digital age could be turned into films, could be repackaged and resold as digital editions, then Marvel turned itself around dramatically as a company.

Martin Seligman has provided a simple three-point recipe for engaging in cognitive reappraisal. Essentially, cognitive reappraisal relies on the idea that you need to change your explanatory style. Explanatory styles refer to how you characteristically explain what happens to you in your life. Seligman suggests that you need to practice three changes to your explanatory style. The first is to shift the explanation from being internal to external. This means saying out loud to yourself that 'it's not always the case that bad things happen because I'm a bad person and I deserve it', but rather that bad events can happen because of chance, and they aren't necessarily your fault. Your default might be to blame yourself; the shift is to attempt to blame the outside world. A more important shift that Seligman emphasises is from a global explanatory style to a specific explanatory style. A global explanatory style occurs when you say that when something has happened that's wrong in your life, it's your fault because you're a bad person and you deserve it, and it indicates that something is terribly wrong with your life; and instead you say 'This is just a small, narrow thing, and it has no implications for the rest of my life'. The final component is to shift from a permanent to an impermanent explanatory style, in other words, saying to yourself that this thing—whatever it happens to be —can be changed, and it's important that it should be changed because that allows me to exert some sense of control over my environment again. These are habits of thought, and as a result they require some considerable degree of work or attention. One way of doing this is by means of journaling. That is, at the end of the day, write down the things that have happened to you that are pleasant and unpleasant. Then, with the unpleasant things, think about explanations for them. Write down your characteristic form of explanation. Then write down how you can change that explanation, focusing on the three dimensions already mentioned, shifting the explanatory style from internal to external, from global to specific and from permanent to impermanent. These are very powerful tools that allow you to change how it is that you characteristically think and feel about what it is that happens in your world.

The Ageing Brain

Senescence—the ageing of the brain—is a pervasive phenomenon in developed and increasingly in developing societies. The media stereotype and common perception of ageing is one of steady decline, loss of cognitive and other faculties, loss of dignity and eventual death. The picture of uniform decay and eventual death is a beguiling and perhaps self-fulfilling one, but it is only a component of a more complex overall picture. A more complex picture is emerging of the changes undergone by the ageing brain, the capabilities and capacities it retains, how the worst effects of ageing might be mitigated and of the continued promise of a fulfilling life that endures, despite the ageing process. The gain in terms of continued personal autonomy and dignity, as well as the reduction in social and economic costs, will be very large indeed if we can ameliorate some of the consequences of ageing. The changes required in terms of behavioural routine to moderate the effects of ageing are quite modest. The trick with ageing is to load the dice as early as one can to slow down the inevitable changes that will occur; this means engaging in behavioural changes that serve to maintain the brain for longer in an optimum state. Another key insight of modern neuroscience, reflected in the idea of life-long neuroplasticity, is that *behaviour changes the brain*, in addition to the brain changing behaviour. The relationship between brain and behaviour is reciprocal, not unidirectional.

Wellbeing, Mindfulness and Positive Brain States

Wellbeing is the subjective sense of feeling good and also of functioning effectively both over time and when challenged by circumstance. Wellbeing also includes the idea of being able to experience negative emotions and being able to manage them appropriately. Being able to deploy good coping skills when tested (such as not losing your temper when provoked by an unreasonable colleague) and controlling impulses when confronted with rewards ('*I WILL ignore the dessert option*') are all central to wellbeing and functioning effectively.

We are, it appears, undergoing something of a 'mindfulness' revolution. Mindfulness is one of those all-pervasive phrases used in a whole variety of differing ways to mean differing things. Some people seem to regard it as a silver bullet that will cure all the ills that befall us; others are much more sceptical. Recently it has become possible to test some of the claims that are being made for mindfulness, defined roughly as a state of being aware of yourself and the pattern of your thoughts and feelings as they traverse your mind while you are in the moment. Mindfulness as a practice owes much to traditional methods of meditation, and meditative practices of differing types have been around for at least some thousands of years, often associated in particular with eastern religious practices such as Buddhism.

I want to suggest here that there is a narrow sense of mindfulness, which has already been hinted at in the first chapter, which we all can profit from. As noted already, our mental lives are very busy. Unprompted, a stream of thoughts and feelings parades itself across our consciousness, and we have little insight from introspection as to the sources of this activity. We also know that cognition did not arise to make us perfect, rational calculators. It happens too quickly and it uses many heuristics to serve the immediate adaptive needs of the present. Being mindful—in this narrow sense—is very useful, because the awareness of the limits to one's cognition can point the way to better ways of making decisions. Similarly, being mindful in this narrow sense is useful for understanding one's own stress response and how to go about ameliorating it. Regrettably, the broader claims about mindfulness as a therapeutic intervention are beyond the space available here. Just remember, though, when someone attempts to sell you a 'mindfulness' solution for whatever ails you, your business or your organisation—ask for the evidence that this is solution works, and works better than other alternatives, and apply the tools for thinking outlined in Chapter 1. There will be few-to-no large-scale, double-blinded, randomised controlled trials available with proper statistical power conducted over the long term to allow you to assess the evidence for the efficacy of mindfulness interventions within organisations. There will be plenty of case studies, however. And this is not to say that mindfulness doesn't work at an organisational level—what we need is lots of evidence that it does. And that it is better than the other alternatives.

Exercise

1. Think back to a personally experienced, stressful event at work. What did you think about it at the time? What do you think about it now? What did you learn from it?

2. Think about a stressor that arises from within your organisation. What can be done to ameliorate the stressor? What steps can you and your organisation take to mitigate the stressor in future? What can you learn from it?
3. Think again of a particular stressor that usually gives you some high degree of stress—such as an important presentation to an important client. Think of the ways that you can engage in cognitive reappraisal of the stressor so that the whole experience becomes easier to deal with.
4. Have you attempted to build some reserve in your life—through regular sleep and regular aerobic exercise in nature?
5. Had Tom Spengler attempted to build resilience in his own life? In his organisation? What steps would you have taken had you been in his place, but knowing what you know now?

Further Reading

Adam S, Bonsang E, Germain S, Perelman S (2007) Retirement and cognitive reserve: a stochastic frontier approach applied to survey data. CREPP Working Paper no. 2007/04, HEC- ULg. http://www.nber.org/chapters/c12983.pdf

American Psychological Association (2017) The road to resilience. http://www.apa.org/helpcenter/road-resilience.aspx

De Quervain DJ, Roozendaal B, McGaugh JL (1998) Stress and glucocorticoids impair retrieval of long-term spatial memory. Nature, 394(6695): 787–790

Kim JJ, Diamond DM (2002) The stressed hippocampus, synaptic plasticity and lost memories. Nature Rev Neurosci., 3:453–462

Lusardi A, Mitchell OS (2006) Financial literacy and planning: Implications for retirement wellbeing. MRRC Working Paper n. 2006–144

Lusardi A, Mitchell OS (2007a) Baby boomer retirement security: The role of planning, financial literacy, and housing wealth. J. Monetary Econ., 54: 205–224

Lusardi A., Mitchell O (2007b) Financial literacy and retirement preparedness. Evidence and implications for financial education. Business economics, 35–44

Lusardi A, Mitchell O (2007c) Financial literacy and retirement planning: New evidence from the rand american life panel. MRRC Working Paper n. 2007–157

O'Mara S, (2015) Why torture doesn't work: The neuroscience of interrogation. Harvard University Press, Cambridge, MA.

Rohwedder S, Willis RJ (2010). Mental retirement. J. Econ. Perspect., 24(1): 119–138. doi: 10.1257/jep.24.1.119.

Seligman MEP (1991). Learned optimism: How to change your mind and your life. Knopf, New York. ISBN 0-671-01911-2. (Paperback reprint edition, Penguin Books, 1998; reissue edition, Free Press, 1998.)

10

Gender, the Brain and Organisations

This chapter takes a brain's-eye view of gender and the brain. It also focuses on behavioural design to enhance gender diversity within organisations.

Few topics give rise to such reliable stereotyping as the topic of gender differences. Differences between male and female behaviour are often thought, often without good evidence, to reflect deep differences in the biology of males and females. Furthermore, observable differences in behaviour are often argued to reflect deep and immutable differences in the structure and function of male and female brains. There is also little doubt that there are deep and pervasive differences within and between societies with regard to how males and females are treated in respect to gender roles, incomes, political power and a whole variety of other variables. Some of these may arise from simple biases regarding gender roles. A wide variety of tests are available now to reveal biases on the parts of males and females with regard to gender roles. The *Implicit Attitude Test* (IAT), developed by psychologists Anthony Greenwald and Mahzarin Banaji, has been widely used to try and reveal latent or hidden associations or social stereotypes that individuals have toward particular targets (such as males, females or individuals from differing ethnic groups; you can take the test at https://implicit.harvard.edu/implicit/takeatest.html and thereby get a sense of your own implicit biases. It's worth doing; you will learn something about yourself. If you can, get someone who knows you well to predict your results before you've done the test). Variations in how people answer the following question are sometimes used to reveal biases within people's thinking about gender roles: a father and son are driving and have a terrible car crash. The

© The Author(s) 2018
S. O'Mara, *A Brain for Business – A Brain for Life*, The Neuroscience of Business, https://doi.org/10.1007/978-3-319-49154-7_10

father is killed instantly, whereas the son is in a critical condition, but alive. The son is rushed to hospital and prepared for a life-saving operation. The surgeon comes into the operating theatre, and on seeing who the patient is, says 'I can't operate on this patient, because that patient is my son!' Now answer the question: who is the surgeon? I first heard this riddle posed by Nilofer Merchant at a management conference. There was an audible pause in the audience before they slowly started to figure out the answer. A married gay male adoptive couple works, but so too does a female surgeon! What was your answer? How long did you take to come up with it?

Do Men and Women Lead Differently?

What does the male brain most resemble in the universe? (Answer below).

'Gender' is a fast and handy way of coding populations and classifying individuals: it is a widely used shortcut because it quickly evokes all sorts of associations about males and females. It allows us to be 'cognitive misers' when we make decisions and choices. But that's all that coding by gender is. There are an infinite number of ways to code populations: height; weight; education; nationality; favourite food preferences; football club preference; music preferences. All fall short because all discard information about individuals in favour of using group membership judgements and stereotypes to allow classification. A better question than '*do men and women lead differently?*' is to ask 'what collection of cognitive and non-cognitive traits (personality, motivation, grit, oratory and so on) in a given context, time and place lead to outcomes that groups who are led value?' This is a very different way of thinking about leadership.

   To assume coding by gender reflects some unchanging and immutable underlying biological reality that describes all we need to know about an individual—that it is a basis for action and choice is simply wrong—and self-evidently so, when you consider the complexity and variation found within and between humans. It is not at all obvious that using gender as a proxy for the traits of leaders is the most useful way of ensuring that the best leaders for the needs of the time are selected. Nor is it the case that the traits of leaders are immutable qualities, independent of time and place, arising irrevocably from gender and brain differences. We need to rethink how we conceive of leaders, and we need to realise that leaders are individuals who may or may not be appropriate to the needs of the time, place and context they are in. And more than that, the cognitive and non-cognitive traits (personality, motivation, grit, oratory and so on) of leaders are not an unchanging given of the male brain or the female brain. They can be learned, honed and sharpened through deliberate and self-conscious practice: this is the great lesson from the behavioural and brain sciences for leaders or aspirant leaders. We humans are capable of learning and profiting from experience and of being changed for the better or worse by our experiences. We might want diversity in leadership for at least two reasons: the first is a moral claim —diversity *is a good thing in itself,* and exclusion of individuals merely because of their membership of one gender is to do their individuality as persons a profound disservice. There is also an instrumental reason, hinted at in Chapter 7 (*Working in Groups*): deliberately promoting diversity allows the possibility of surfacing useful and important informa- tion that otherwise would be unavailable to the organisation. Given these reasons, we need to change how we think about gender and leadership. We need to shift the focus to the traits and skills needed to fulfil the demands of the position. We need to design evaluation procedures that are benchmarked according to objective standards, and we need to design processes in organisations that select for skills and traits and that set aside gender as the selection variable. To *not* change is the easy thing to do—it is the approach of the cognitive miser—but who ever said anything worthwhile was easy? And, of course, the male brain most resembles the female brain—this was not a trick question!

As noted above, gender is merely a means of coding a population. There is and there continues to be a major debate about the relationship between gender and brain function, and there are lots of things that one can say about this. The first really is to start with some important distinctions. People's gender identity, their gender expression, their biological sex and their sexual orientation can all vary, and we should therefore not engage in stereotyping of individuals for ethical reasons, but also for the simple reason that stereo- typing involves loss of granularity of information about individuals and their capacities and abilities. We also need to avoid an important mistake, which is commonly made, which is that, because there might or might not be sex-related differences in the brains of males and females, this difference somehow then explains behavioural differences that might arise between males and females. The science simply does not allow us to make this conclusion. In an important and comprehensive brain imaging study con- ducted with males and females, Daphna Joel and colleagues (2015) show that perhaps the best way to conceive of brains, irrespective of whether they are male or female, is that they are made up of 'mosaics' of features, some of which might appear more frequently in female brains and some of which might appear more frequently in male brains. But it turns out that coding or sorting these data on male/female lines is possibly one of the least interesting ways of understanding what happens in terms of brain differences, because human brains, as a population, cannot be ascribed to one or other of two distinct coding classes, namely the male brain or the female brain. There are brains that look like the brains of males walking around in bodies that are biologically female, and there are brains that look female walking around in bodies that look biologically male. We therefore need to avoid treating individual humans as anything other than individuals with their own complex psychological makeup, instantiated within a brain that cannot be distinctly classified as male or female, but that happens to be housed within a body that, depending on its gross surface features, can be classified as male or female. For those interested in reading into these issues more deeply, Cahill (2017) is highly recommended.

Male/Female Cognitive Differences

There has been a century or so long tradition of searching for differences between males and females in respect to performance on a variety of cognitive tasks. Often, when such differences are found, they are given the '*men are from Mars and women are from Venus*' treatment, where extreme stereotyping is used to generate laughter, to sell books or to act as clickbait on websites. The point needs to be emphasised that performance on cognitive tasks, if conducted at a population level, will lead to a distribution of responses, with some individuals being closer to one end of the tail of the distribution, and others being at the other end, with a large group in between. In other words, for any given cognitive and behavioural trait, there will be males and females above or below each other when a gender-based comparison is made.

An important large-scale study by Daniel Wright and Elin Skagerberg of empathising and systemising in 5186 male and female participants illustrates this point well. Empathising is key to our social lives and social interactions, as it allows you to identify with the mental states of others—their thoughts and feelings, and to respond to these mental states with appropriate emotions. Systemising, by contrast, is a drive focused on regularities and predictability, and it manifests itself especially in a preference to analyse, explore and construct systems. Males are often regarded as being lower in empathising and higher in systemising than females. Wright and Skagerberg (2012) summarise their data as follows: '*Females had on average higher empathizing scores and males had on average higher systemizing scores. If a female-male pair was chosen at random, the female would have the higher empathizing score about two-thirds of the time, and the males would have the higher systemizing score about two-thirds of the time.*' This is an important way of thinking about these differences: we can select given individuals of any gender within the tails of the particular distribution, and for a given trait, there will be individuals of the other gender who will score above and below them—and this despite the average of the two distributions differing! The key points are, of course, to think about dispersal around means of any given distribution and to focus on individual differences, not mean or average group differences.

Other trait distributions may follow the bell-shaped distribution pattern, and in turn there may be sex-linked differences, which are as yet ill understood. For example, we see, with respect to psychopathology, that females tend to suffer greater rates of major depressive disorder than males and that males tend to suffer greater rates of attention deficit disorder, psychosis and autistic spectrum disorders compared with females. It needs to be emphasised that these are observational data. They do not speak causally, as far as our current state of knowledge allows us to do, to any underlying biological mechanisms in terms of male/female differences. After all, there are females who have autistic spectrum disorder, and there are males who become depressed.

The most reliable male/female difference in cognition has to do with three-dimensional visuospatial reasoning. Reliably, differences can be found between males and females on three-dimensional tasks that involve complex aspects of spatial cognition. However, the differences are found for a single tail of the distribution (the right hand side) where it tends to be the case that there are a greater number of males who perform very well in spatial tasks compared with females. When you look at the distribution as a whole, it is also the case that there are many females who outperform males on spatial tasks. Therefore, the old joke that men don't listen and women can't read maps can't be taken seriously as a scientific statement about the essential differences between male and female cognition. There is a further and important point here. Several lines of data suggest that these observed differences are profoundly malleable. By this I mean they are subject to experience-dependent modification. It appears that a simple intervention, namely playing a three-dimensional video action game for an hour a day for five days is enough to remove a pre-existing difference between males and females in spatial cognition, such that female performance is statistically indistinguishable from that of males (Feng and colleagues 2007). Furthermore, in an especially clever study, Moshe Hoffman and colleagues (2011) contrasted male and female performance in matrilineal and patrilineal societies in two distinct tribes in Northeast India (the Khasi and the Karbi). Females were at a disadvantage in patrilineal societies on three-dimensional puzzle games, taking longer to solve complex three-dimensional puzzles in a patrilineal society. But they were equally good as males in the matrilineal society. In other words, there was no difference in male/female performance in spatial cognition in females who grew up in a matrilineal society. Remarkably, the data also appear to indicate that male performance in the matrilineal society is better than male performance in the patrilineal society. In other words, in societies where females take a more dominant role in power relations, male performance is actually enhanced relative to societies where females do not have a predominant role in the exercise of power relations.

The key point to make here is that gender gaps at the population level in cognition are real; it is possible to find them, especially in the case of spatial cognition, but those gender gaps do not reflect an immutable, unchanging, underlying biological essence in terms of brain structure and function that permanently and enduringly differentiates males and females. Rather, these different properties of male and female brains arise, at least in part, as a result of experience and can be modified through appropriate interventions. In a different demonstration of the power of these interventions, Sheryl Sorby and Beverley Baartmans (2000) have focused on gender gaps in male/female graduation rates in engineering. They find that three-dimensional visualisation of complex objects can be difficult initially for some females training to be engineers. However, a simple course of spatial cognition training, focused on visualisation of objects in three dimensions, the transformation of objects in three dimensions, imagining and building mirror images of objects, has a profound effect on female performance during training to become engineers. Sorby says 'If you start with 100 women, you'd expect 50 to graduate as engineers . . . if we give them this intervention, 80 will graduate from engineering' bringing their graduation rates up to those of their male counterparts. Results like this really are very striking and very heartening. They make it very difficult to maintain an 'essentialist' view of the differences between males and females, where cognition is concerned. They also emphasise that devising interventions and testing experimentally the outcomes of those interventions can markedly and materially affect how individuals will perform on particular tasks. They also should help us to break down male/female stereotyping differences, where cognition is concerned.

A related issue is that of bias and gender roles. There are regular media stories about the 'male brain' versus the 'female brain', and these stories have given rise to myths about male and female performance. And myths they are, because these stories are based on what are non-causal, non-mechanistic observational and epidemiological data (even if they are accompanied by dazzlingly beautiful images of brains) and report group average differences—they are usually not based on experimental or interventional data. They do not address the issue of individual performance. Recent studies show that attempts at de-biasing for race or gender do not stick—they tend to last approximately a day or so (Forscher et al. 2016). There is good news however—there are important and straightforward structural changes that can be made in the workplace that will attenuate gender biases and will do so quite dramatically over time. A straightforward example is the composition of players in orchestras: these were all-male affairs until blind-tested auditions, where players were tested behind curtains. Uniformly, when this strategy is adopted, the male gender composition bias of orchestras disappears, and orchestras become mixed, based solely on performance criteria.

Environmental Design

The next time you are out for a walk, consider the environment that you find yourself in. You want to cross the road but you may find railings preventing you crossing before the traffic lights, dimpled tiles with a dip for a wheelchair and auditory signals for people with restricted vision that they are at the appropriate crossing point. These are examples of simple behavioural design cues provided in the environment to drive our behaviour in particular ways. A movement known as the 'nudge movement' has developed around the idea that the 'choice architecture' of our environment can help move our behaviour in the direction of desired outcomes and away from less desirable outcomes (Thaler and Sunstein 2008; Thaler 2015). There are many examples of this: opt-out rather than opt-in organ donations systems; insurance forms where you sign at the top asserting that you will not engage in a fraudulent return rather than at the end; the layouts of cafeterias and shops that are designed to drive you either to or away from eating fruit, or perhaps somewhat less desirable foods. These are all examples of 'behavioural designs', designs that are focused on how we interact with the environment and also with each other, to generate particular behaviours. Behavioural design can be, as I hope to show below, a very powerful for moving behaviours towards desired outcomes.

Attitudes and Behaviour

It is often claimed that attitudes drive behaviour rather than the other way around. Behavioural design takes the view that attitudes follow behaviour, or are modified as a result of behaviour, rather than the attitude itself having primacy. In recent years, tests of implicit bias have shown that humans of every type manifest biases toward or against others of the same sex or the opposite sex; same ethnicity or some other ethnicity; some arbitrarily-designated in-group versus an arbitrarily-designated out-group. These implicit biases are pervasive and may lie at the core of at least some of the asymmetric outcomes that we see when we look at gender gaps, or ethnic gaps or class-based gaps in performance. Many studies have focused on how these implicit biases might be eliminated (e.g. Finnegan et al. 2015). In one particularly powerful study by Forscher and colleagues (2016) a particular focus was made on interventions against racism. Forscher and his co-workers concluded 'We tested nine implicit bias interventions. All worked immediately, zero worked after a day'. This, on the face of it, is a real problem. If the best interventions that we have to ameliorate the effects of racism show only short-acting effects, then society at large has a problem. There are all sorts of potential reasons for why implicit bias interventions might fail. One is very simple: it is a confusion of cause and effect where behavioural outcomes are concerned. The idea is that we shift the bias and that by adjusting the bias this will adjust behaviour. It may well be the case that shifting behaviour will shift the bias.

Another reason is that acquiring new habits, either of behaviour or mind, is difficult. New habits are not 'sticky'. In one particularly telling set of experiments (Lally et al. 2010), which focused on the length of time it took volunteers to acquire a new habit such as doing some daily exercise, eating a portion of fruit and the like, a huge variation in performance was found. The authors state, 'The time it took participants to reach 95% of their asymptote of automaticity ranged from 18 to 254 days, indicating considerable variation in how long it takes people to limit of automaticity, and highlighting that it can take a very long time. Missing one opportunity to perform the behaviour did not materially affect the habit formation process. Data like these should give one pause. If well-motivated volunteers who were tracked over a substantial period of time (up to 254 days) found it difficult to adjust a single behaviour such that it became a habit, how much more difficult will it be to shift a whole set of constellations of thoughts, feelings and biases with respect to members of some out-group? The answer is very difficult indeed. We could wonder if this is simply a matter of cognitive control. In other words, we should be focused on keeping the appropriate rule for behaviour in mind and then obeying that rule. Would that that were so easy. In a particularly dramatic real-world study, Shai Danziger and their colleagues (2011) focused on how judges in court make decisions on like-for-like traffic offences. The punishment prescribed under law is of a particular type, but with latitude available for the judge to apply some legal discretion. The results were astonishingly clear. The proportion of decisions that were favourable was highest in the morning, showing a steady decline to just before lunch, when the chance of a favourable decision fell to approximately zero. After lunch it rose to the same level as in the morning and fell towards the afternoon break, and then it would rise dramatically after the afternoon break to the same level again as in the morning, but fall precipitously towards the end of the day. So here you have an example of well-trained individuals with lots of experience, with a rule-book that gives order and direction to their decisions, but that, crucially, allows them discretion to give favourable or unfavourable judgements, and what we find is that the proportion of favourable judgements varies directly in relation to how rested the judge is, giving life to the old phrase from the USA that justice is '*what the judge ate for breakfast*'.

The implications of data like these are relatively straightforward: cognitive control over decision-making is very hard, even in highly educated, well-trained individuals, where circumstances are similar from time to time. The key point here is that the behaviour is held more or less constant, but the outcome varies depending on how tired the judge is and the period of time since the last rest break. How much greater a difficulty is then presented when we are expecting individuals, as the result of a short intervention, to permanently shift their decision-making processes? The key lesson, therefore, is that we should not make the mistake of locating decision-making solely within the individual; instead we must design the environment to provide the necessary decision-making supports. Consider the example that we started this chapter with. You want to cross the road, but because of street furniture design you can only cross at crossing points that the city planners will allow you to cross at. We can use similar forms of principles to make design changes in how we make decisions about which employees to recruit into particular positions.

In her important book, '*What Works: Gender Equality by Design*', Iris Bohnet (2016) invites us to consider a well-known example. The orchestras of the world historically had few female players. The Boston Symphony Orchestra, for example, in the early 1950s had fewer than 5% female players. In 2010 the orchestra was comprised of about 40–45% female players. The natural question to ask is 'What happened?' Did the men suddenly take on board the lessons of the women's liberation movement? Did fewer men apply to become players in the orchestra? Did some happy accident happen that wiped out or removed many of the male players? Of course not. Behavioural change happened first, and attitudes followed, and a simple piece of behavioural design changed everything. This was the use of blind auditions, where prospective players applying for a position in the orchestra were auditioned behind a curtain or a screen, so that their gender identity was unknown to the selection committee. This caused a dramatic shift in terms of who was employed as an orchestra player. It also suggests that because of simple bias, orchestras hitherto were under-sampling the talent pool available to them, and when this bias was simply obviated by a curtain, the talent pool was greatly expanded. It must have been quite something to see the faces of the selectors when they realised that their new lead soloist on the cello was going to be a female.

Are there other places that we can engage in behavioural design? The answer is yes, there are many. Bohnet and colleagues (2012), in an important paper entitled 'When Performance Trumps Gender Bias: Joint versus Separate Evaluation', show that when male and female assessors consider male and female applicants, where the only critical variable that is changed is the gender of the applicant, that a considerable gender bias worms its way into decision-making for occupational positions. This bias disappears when the applications are considered jointly or in a pooled fashion rather than serially. The implication here is very straightforward: to de-bias, you must put in a behavioural decision change. The changes are straightforward: establish an objective benchmark for performance, and always do joint evaluations. Never allow a situation to arise where individuals are compared against benchmarks located within one person's head. These benchmarks must be stated and they must be explicit, and when comparisons of one actual person are made against another actual person, the biasing effect of gender tends to fall dramatically. The implication here is straightforward: locate changes in the design of the system of assessment and evaluation, and not in attempting to change attitudes or behaviour. A focus on shifting attitudes makes what is known as the 'fundamental attribution error'. It locates the locus of change solely within the individual rather than in the social and behavioural context that the individual sits within. Focusing on design changes of this type prevents unidirectional thinking that attitudes cause behaviour and allows the idea that attitudes might change as a result of behaviour. In other words, changing the environment, changing the decision supports and structures, changes outcomes, which in turn changes attitudes. Objectively, it must be the case that the new lead soloist is better because you have judged that lead soloist to be better in the absence of any other information other than the pure behavioural performance of the individual.

The Perils of Interviewing

It is clear from more than 50 years of research in occupational psychology that in unstructured interviews we will choose people that we like based on person judgement biases (e.g., Dipboye 1997; Wiesner and Cronshaw 1988). We have already encountered these in Chapter six on how we perceive other individuals. We choose on the basis of how it is that the person makes us feel at interview, and we will use proxies for performance, like which Ivy League university they attended or the like. We know also from research conducted in a variety of domains that the best predictors of on-the-job performance include variables such as conscientiousness, motivation, previous track record, mastery of a domain, expertise and similar factors. Therefore, the challenge in assessment interviews is to devise standardised, structured, objectively scored interview procedures, where individuals are evaluated in comparison to each other and are hired or promoted in batches. Ideally, demographic information should be removed from job applications and task-oriented predictive tests and problems, along with structured interviews, be used to evaluate candidates. And the real word of warning is that unstructured interviews should never be used.

Implementing Behavioural Design

Implementing behavioural design changes in complex environments is difficult, but there are things that can be done. If telephone screening is being used for candidates, a relatively straightforward change is to use a filter to remove high and low frequencies from candidates' voices over the phone, removing the bias that both males and females have in favour of lower register and bass-accented voices. A useful exercise at this point would be to consider your own occupational environment and to generate a short list of the changes that could be implemented that would facilitate de-biasing in terms of assessment for occupational selection and promotion. One way of ensuring that behavioural design changes are implemented in the appropriate way can be taken from the aerospace industry. This is through the use of carefully designed checklists from which data can be harvested to ensure that design procedures have been followed. A particularly useful guide is Atul Gawande's book 'The Checklist Manifesto'. The use of simple and straight-forward checklists will reduce working memory load dramatically and thereby obviate the issue of cognitive control (and were they to be adopted by the courts, it might result in more uniform sentencing outcomes). A checklist will facilitate the retrieval of information from long-term memory; it will help organise tasks appropriately; it provides a focus on ensuring that the appropriate processes have been implemented; it facilitates standardisa-tion and record-keeping and allows deviations from processes and procedures to be tracked. An appropriately designed set of checklists within a sufficiently large organisation will allow that organisation to make comparisons in processes, procedures and outcomes across its differing geographical locales, where they are performing essentially the same task. In an assessment situa-tion, a set of checklists might revolve around: first of all, standardising candidate selection so that all candidates are compared against the same set of criteria. During interviews, a checklist will ensure that the same question is asked in the same order by the same person of each candidate during the interview process. And then, during the selection process, the checklist will ensure that candidates are compared with each other on a like-for-like basis rather than forcing the interviewers to rely on a suite of biases, heuristics and salient points from the interview that may or may not be predictive of anything in particular where on the job performance is concerned. Checklists, of course, come with caveats. In a design context, they would require some degree of experimentation and testing to ensure that they are focused appropriately on generating de-biased outcomes and therefore the selection of the very best possible candidate for the position at hand.

Changing Behaviour

Changing the behaviour of other people is difficult, in part because there are many myths that need to be tackled. The first is that education or well-intended interventions will change behaviour. Most people think that if others are educated about an issue they'll change. If this were true, there would be no smokers or anti-vaccination campaigners in the world. In other words, knowledge and knowing is not enough, and is especially not enough when people engage in identity-defensive cognition or identity-congruent cognition, where the outcome of thinking is to reinforce their membership of a particular social group, and to reinforce aspects of their own personal identity which may be bound up in the particular cause that they have committed themselves to. The second myth that needs slaying is that you need to change attitudes to change behaviour. Rather than assuming there is a unidirectional causality, attitudes lead to behaviour; we should take this relationship as bidirectional: that attitudes follow behaviour and that attitudes are caused by behaviour. If we survey people about their attitudes, we can't accurately predict, for example, how they will vote. Why is this? It is because social norms within the person's environment are a significant moderator of their behaviour, independently of their expressed attitudes. Thus, we need to design processes, policies and procedures in workplaces, organisations and institutions to facilitate and de-bias decision-making for occupational recruitment, selection and advancement in particular, but for organisational decisions of great moment in general. The last myth, then, is straightforward: we assume that people know what motivates them to take action. This leads us to assume that we think we know what really motivates us on any particular occasion to engage in a particular behaviour, but we don't really. The great motivators around us are in fact social comparison and social norms. When we go into a crowded room with seats and we see others sitting, we will sit. If an alarm goes off within the room, we will wait for the majority of people to make a movement before heading for the fire exit. There is great behavioural inertia present in what we do as a result of the social circumstances that we find ourselves in. Thus, if we see one person behaving in a particular way, we are more likely ourselves to do the same thing as well.

A Story About Reds and Greens

Finally, we will finish this chapter on bias by examining occupational outcomes for blobs of colour in a two-dimensional world. Our blobs are red and our blobs are green, and they are recruited to work in a large organisation to do similar kinds of jobs. Now, there is one crucial difference between reds and greens: reds have a slight propensity to fantasise, to engage in self-talk about how wonderful a particular outcome might be. Greens don't do this. Greens, instead, think much more about the probabilities of a particular outcome occurring, rather than thinking much about how wonderful the outcome itself will be. So what happens? Reds are slightly deluded, or self-confident, or whatever, but they start to apply for promotion as soon as they possibly can, because the outcome of the promotion will be so wonderful, and they're going to fail. Greens, on the other hand, wait until they are ready to apply for a promotion, because they are focused on the probability of the outcome. This way of thinking emphasises that they will succeed and want to ensure that they don't fail. And what happens? One of the reds goes up against one of the greens for a particularly desired promotion. The red has tried three times already and succeeds on this occasion. This is the first occasion for the green to try for promotion, and it fails. The question is why? We can think of all sorts of reasons, but one set of reasons is fairly straightforward. Our red blob has had several rounds of feedback from prior failures, whereas our green hasn't. Furthermore, red has demonstrated motivation and desire, a hunger to get up the greasy pole, whereas green thinks hard work will demonstrate motivation (and this isn't true). Can you think of other reasons why this might happen? Which of these rough categories do you find yourself in?

Exercises

1. Examine the riddle used in the opening of the chapter. Create other versions of it where males and females are used in counter-stereotypical occupational roles (e.g. male beauticians; female car mechanics; male childcare workers; female burglars). Start by listing occupational roles that you typically associate with males or females.
2. Write down the cognitive attributes and personality attributes (These are generally and empirically agreed to be the Big Five—openness to experience, conscientiousness, extraversion, agreeableness and neuroticism) you believe are associated with the following occupations:

Surgeon
Criminal Lawyer
Accountant
Life Coach
Football Coach
Olympic Athlete
Chief Executive Officer
Teacher

Barista
Biomedical Researcher
Publisher

3. Now write F (female) or M (male) if you strongly associate these occupations with female or males. Write F & M if you have no strong association for these occupations.
4. Now think about when you did 3 above. Did the label you applied happen because you could readily think of an example for the category—a person or two that you could recall explicitly? If so, you are probably using the 'availability heuristic' (Chapter 4) to guide your association—the example or examples that spring to mind.
5. Now, go to your favourite search engine and do an image search for each of these occupations, first as listed, and then either as 'male surgeon' or 'female surgeon', and so on. Now, what do you think? Have your mental shortcuts lead you astray?
6. What do you imagine Tom Spengler's views on diversity might be?

Further Reading

Bohnet I (2016) What works: Gender equality by design. Harvard University Press, Cambridge, MA.

Bohnet I, Bazerman, MH, Van Geen, A (2012) When performance trumps gender bias: Joint versus separate evaluation. HKS Working Paper no. RWP12-009, https://papers.ssrn.com/sol3/papers.cfm?abstract_id=2087613

Cahill L (2017) An issue whose time has come: Sex/Gender influences on nervous system function. J. Neurosci. Res., 95: Spc1–Spc1, 1–791. http://onlinelibrary.wiley.com/doi/10.1002/jnr.v95.1-2/issuetoc

Danziger S, Levav J, Avnaim-Pesso L (2011) Extraneous factors in judicial decisions. Proc. Natl. Acad. Sci., 108(6889–6892). doi: 10.1073/pnas.1018033108.

Dipboye RL (1997) Structured selection interviews: Why do they work? Why are they underutilized? In: Anderson N, Herriott P (eds) International handbook of selection and assessment, J Wiley, London. 455–474

Feng J, Spence I, Pratt J (2007). Playing an action video game reduces gender differences in spatial cognition. Psychol Sci., 18(850–855). doi: 10.1111/j.1467-9280.2007.01990.x.

Finnegan E, Oakhill J, Garnham A (2015). Counter-stereotypical pictures as a strategy for overcoming spontaneous gender stereotypes. Front. Psychol., 6:1291. doi: 10.3389/fpsyg.2015.01291.

Forscher PS, Lai CK, Axt JR, Ebersole CR, Herman M, Devine PG, Nosek BA (under revision). A meta-analysis of change in implicit bias. Psychol. Bull., Paper & materials: https://osf.io/awz2p/

Gawande, A (2011) The checklist manifesto. Picador, London.

Greenwald AG, Banaji MR (2013) Blindspot: Hidden biases of good people. Delacorte Press, New York.

Hoffman M, Gneezy U, List JA (2011). Nurture affects gender differences in spatial abilities. Proc. Natl. Acad. Sci., 108(14786–14788). doi: 10.1073/pnas.1015182108.

Joel D, Berman Z, Tavor I, Wexler N, Gaber O, Stein Y, Assaf Y (2015) Sex beyond the genitalia: The human brain mosaic. Proc Natl Acad Sci U S A., 112(50): 15468–15473. http://doi.org/10.1073/pnas.1509654112.

Lally P, Van Jaarsveld CHM, Potts HWW, Wardle J (2010). How are habits formed: Modelling habit formation in the real world. Eur. J. Soc. Psychol., 40: 998–1009. doi: 10.1002/ejsp.674.

Sorby SA, Baartmans BJ (2000) The development and assessment of a course for enhancing the 3-D spatial visualization skills of first year engineering students. J. Eng. Educ., 301–307. http://vanderbilt.edu/gised/wp-content/uploads/Sorby_DevelopmentAssessmentCourse-Enhancing3DSpatialVisualizationSkills Engineering.pdf. (see also: Andrew Curry, 2016, Men Are Better At Maps Until Women Take This Course. http://nautil.us/issue/32/space/men-are-better-at-maps-until-women-take-this-course).

Thaler RH (2015) Misbehaving: The making of behavioral economics. Allen Lane, London.

Thaler RH, Sunstein CR (2008) Nudge: Improving decisions about health, wealth, and happiness. Yale University Press, New Haven, CT.

Wiesner WH, Cronshaw SF (1988) A meta-analytic investigation of the impact of interview format and degree of structure on the validity of the employment interview. J. Occup. Organ. Psychol., 61(4): 275–290.

Wright DB, Skagerberg EM (2012) Measuring empathizing and systemizing with a large us sample. *PLoS ONE*, 7(2): e31661. doi: 10.1371/journal.pone.0031661.

11

Concluding Scenario Analysis

Tom Spengler found himself lying in his hospital bed with lots of time to think, reflect, read and learn. The brush with death and the evident lack of people beyond his family who came to visit him deeply affected him. Where were all his friends now? The sad truth was that he had few friends—he had spent so long treating others as mere instruments there to assist in his own path to glory that he had forgotten the importance of friends and family, and similarly, too, his health. Smoking was not something that encouraged either heart or lung health—his heart in particular, as he had just discovered. A kind friend—one of the very few he still had—who worked in a publishing house, somehow acquired and passed him an early draft of this book.

Both Chapter 1 and Exercises were missing, so he had to draw the lessons out for himself. He starting with a self-scripting exercise—one that was painful, but valuable, as he asked himself how he could change for the better as a leader, follower, person, father and husband in the future. Yes—he had a family—and had given them little thought in his pursuit of his own self-defined glory—a glory that he now understood would have been marked by the human version of dominance displays and petty exercises of power. He hadn't asked himself whom these were designed to impress. He was out of it permanently, of course—the new business had no need of him either, as he had made it equally clear that he had no need of his new colleagues. He had forgotten the simple rules of reciprocity in human interaction—that people will treat you as you treat them. Trying to take the perspective of others was something he would do more of in the future. Bringing people along, using

© The Author(s) 2018

S. O'Mara, *A Brain for Business – A Brain for Life*, The Neuroscience of Business, https://doi.org/10.1007/978-3-319-49154-7_11

open, deliberative processes that allow all involved to feel like they are contributing meaningfully, was also something to try for the future.

Looking out for his own head and heart health was also top of his new to-do list. Getting regular aerobic exercise and finding a neighbourhood walking partner using an app that he was going to think about getting commercialised would do the trick. Smoking was off his list now, and practicing some deep relaxation, getting regular sleep, and even a little mindfulness was where he was at now. But what should he do now? Tom was lucky—and he now knew it—he'd been given a decent pay-off, and he held shares in the new merged GLH Pharma. Does some aspect of post-traumatic growth beckon? Tom hoped that it might. So, too, did his family.

Exercise

1. Imagine you are Tom Spengler. Make out a list of the cognitive biases that you displayed in the period up to and during the merger process.
2. Imagine again that you are Tom Spengler. Knowing what you know now, what would you differently if given the chance to do it all over again?
3. Think of a circumstance where you have made a series of poor judgements. What would you differently now, knowing what you know now?
4. Is change possible for Tom? Will anything enduring come from the whole episode, or is it likely that he will simply go back to the way he was before?
5. What can he do to make sure positive and desirable change occurs in the way he lives his life?
6. What lessons do you draw from this book for positive and possible behavioural change? Now—write out the implementation intentions associated with this change—the set of concrete behavioural steps required to turn thought into consistent action.

Index

© The Author(s) 2018
S. O'Mara, *A Brain for Business – A Brain for Life*, The Neuroscience
of Business, https://doi.org/10.1007/978-3-319-49154-7

Printed by Printforce, the Netherlands